# CRUX

## Daily Lenten Meditations

Fr. Columba Jordan, CFR

ASCENSION

West Chester, Pennsylvania

Ascension
PO Box 1990
West Chester, PA 19380
1-800-376-0520
ascensionpress.com

Cover art: Chris Lewis (BARITUS Catholic)
Book design: Stella Ziegler

Printed in the United States of America.

ISBN: 979-8-89276-146-8

# CONTENTS

# INTRODUCTION

Welcome to *Crux: Daily Lenten Meditations*. This devotional book is a component of *Crux: A Lenten Journey of Surrender*, presented by Fr. Columba Jordan, CFR. Inspired by a holistic view of body and soul, the *Crux* program will guide you through Lent by balancing physical and spiritual disciplines that will help you encounter your weaknesses with mercy and surrender it all to God.

The devotional you are holding, which features daily reflections from Fr. Columba and artwork by Chris Lewis, is intended to help you and your family draw closer to Jesus during the Lenten season by letting you build a habit of daily Scripture reading and prayer, keeping your eyes fixed on your Lenten goals, and reminding you of your true identity in Christ.

## Lenten Disciplines with the *Crux* Program

Lent is an opportunity to face physical and spiritual challenges that, when offered to Christ in sincerity of heart and will, can help us grow in holiness and reinforce our identities as his beloved children. Fr. Columba encourages you to balance the needs of your body and those of your soul by participating in four Lenten challenges—two physical and two spiritual.

*Physical Disciplines*

- Fasting: abstaining from certain foods, beverages, and treats

- Physical exercise: daily movement and workouts (in accordance with your physical ability and fitness level)

*Spiritual Disciplines*

- Spiritual reading: encountering God through Scripture each day

- Prayer: setting intentional time aside for personal conversation with God

The physical challenges are designed for everyone, no matter their season of life or ability. The dietary fast will look different for everyone depending on age and health.

This devotional is a key part of your daily spiritual reading throughout Lent and will guide you through select passages from Scripture that will help you receive and rest in God's Word.

## The *Crux* Daily Reflections

The reflections in this book will accompany you through Lent and are intended for daily use.

Each reflection is broken down into three parts:

### Read

The devotional leads you through the entire Gospel of Mark—the narrative of Jesus' public ministry and his Passion, death, and Resurrection. For weeks 1–5, the Sunday readings follow the Sunday Mass readings for Lent Cycle A, while Palm Sunday and Easter continue your journey through the Gospel of Mark. Each day features a specific passage (or passages) from Scripture and a key verse that serves as a focal point for the day's reflection. We recommend reading the selected Scripture verses first before reading Fr. Columba's reflection.

### Reflect

Through Fr. Columba's reflections, you will dive into the themes from the day's Scripture reading and explore how it helps us understand our identity as God's beloved children, the meaning of Christ's sacrifice, and the call of Christian discipleship. Drawing from personal experience and the wisdom of the Church, Fr. Columba will help you uncover the deeper significance and connections we find in God's Word.

### Respond

Each daily reflection ends with a challenge, journal prompt, or guided prayer that will let you carry forward what you have read into your daily life, putting Fr. Columba's reflections into action.

## Getting the Most Out of This Devotional

### Community

Community is a key component for this journey through Lent. Fr. Columba focuses on many daily challenges that he encourages us to participate in. Through community, we allow for an opportunity to grow both in prayer and friendship with others on this shared journey to heaven.

The ideal is for a parish or small group to take up the Crux and journey together as a community. You can find out how to provide journals to a large parish group, at AscensionPress. com/Crux-Parish-Resources, which also includes information about how to buy in bulk, run parish events, and implement the free Sunday videos within your community.

If you are not able to experience *Crux* as a whole parish, consider a small group setting where you can join in community to help one another remain accountable during the season. Download the Small Group Resource for discussion questions and guidance on leading a small group within your parish at AscensionPress. com/Crux-Parishes. You can use the devotional as a family or get together with a group of friends to discuss how God is calling you to define your identity within him during Lent. Bulk pricing is also available for small groups.

You can take this journey through Lent even if you are not meeting in a group or talking about it with friends or family. *Crux* is well suited for use by individuals. Remember that you are not alone: Catholics all over the country are on the same journey. This devotional is a place for you to speak to God and to hear and see all that he has shown you.

### *Videos*

The *Crux* Lenten program includes free weekly videos featuring Fr. Columba, which are available on the Ascension App (either on your mobile device or on the web at AscensionPress.com/app). If you're wanting to delve deeper into the Lenten experience, you can subscribe to a premium subscription (7-day free trial or $4.99 for 90 days of access) for daily videos to accompany you on your Lenten journey. Through Fr. Columba's guidance, humor, wisdom, and prayer, you will find fresh insights into the profound love that the Lord instilled in us at our baptism, defining our identity. Through Jesus' Passion, death, and Resurrection, we are being called to bear witness to our Lord's mercy.

### The Crux *Tracker Journal*

This devotional can be paired with the *Crux: A Lenten Journey of Surrender* tracker journal that encourages you to actively track your daily fasting, workout, reading, and prayer disciplines throughout Lent. With a planner-like design and plenty of space for writing, the *Crux* journal calls you to partake in one or all of the challenges to encourage fortitude and sacrifice during the Lenten season.

### Family Components

This devotional includes family resources for each full week of Lent. These resources feature prayers, inspirational quotes, challenges, and other activities that align thematically with the *Crux*'s four Lenten disciplines and this devotional's daily reflections. They are a helpful way for you to journey toward Christ's Resurrection together as a family and keep this season of fasting, penance, almsgiving, and prayer centered on the loving sacrifice of Jesus.

## Tips for Praying with Scripture

### To Begin: Prepare

When you are praying with Scripture, open your Bible and read the passage once. Get familiar with the words. Then, slowly read the text a second time. Pay attention to how you feel as you read. When the text sets a scene, enter the scene with one of the individuals mentioned. You may consider reading the text a third time to highlight what stands out to you.

*ARRR: Acknowledge, Relate, Receive, Respond*

The "ARRR" method is a simple approach to prayer.

1. **Acknowledge:** You have sat with God's Word. You have entered the scene. Now, when you feel that God is saying something to you, acknowledge what stirs within you. Pay attention to your thoughts, feelings, and desires. These are important.

2. **Relate:** After acknowledging what is going on in your heart, relate that to God. Don't just think about your thoughts, feelings, and desires. Don't just think about God or how God might react. Relate to God. Tell him how you feel. Tell him what you think. Tell him what you want. Share all your thoughts, feelings, and desires with God. Share everything with him.

3. **Receive:** Once you have shared everything with God, receive from him. Listen to what he is telling you. It could be a subtle voice you hear. It could be a memory that pops up. Maybe he invites you to reread the Scripture passage. Perhaps he invites you into a still, restful silence. Trust that God is listening to you, and receive what he wants to share with you.

4. **Respond:** Now respond to him. Your response could be continuing your conversation with God. It could be resolving to do something. It could be tears or laughter. Respond to what you are receiving.

## Write It Down

Keep a record of your prayer this Lent. It does not have to be lengthy; it could be a single word, a sentence or two about what God told you, or it could be about how the day's reflection struck you. However you do it, taking note of your prayer will help you walk closer to God this Lent.

The *Crux* tracker journal is a perfect resource for writing down your thoughts, feelings, and inspirations throughout your Lenten journey.

## Commit

As you dedicate yourself to prayer this Lent, there is no better safeguard than a good plan. We recommend the five Ws as a method of prayer planning. Every Sunday, look at your calendar and write out your plan for the next six days, answering the following questions: When? Where? What? Who? and Why?

- WHEN will I spend time with Jesus?
- WHERE will I spend time with Jesus?
- WHAT are Jesus and I going to do together?
- WHO will hold me accountable for my time with Jesus?
- WHY am I prioritizing my time with Jesus?

Making a commitment is the first step in transforming your prayer life.

Watch Fr. Columba's free weekly Lenten reflections as a small group or parish.

*Ash*

WEDNESDAY

# Surrender

*Read Mark 1:1–11*

*"A voice came from heaven, 'You are my beloved Son; with you I am well pleased.'"*

## Reflect

Welcome to the "first" day of Lent. This season, our goal is to grow closer to God through surrender—and we're going to do this by choosing to do hard things. Why? Because doing hard things—things that stretch us, things that challenge us, things that we would rather avoid—is what helps us recognize our limitations. Doing hard things helps us encounter our weaknesses, which is precisely where God wants to meet us. Doing hard things teaches us to surrender to Christ in faith.

One of the biggest obstacles to real growth in Christ is the opposite of surrender: namely, self-reliance. When we try to do everything on our own, we get in the way of the work Christ wants to do in us and for us. If we want to make progress in our relationship with God, we first need to get out of our own way by relinquishing control and allowing God to act.

To that end, I'm challenging you to take on four disciplines throughout Lent, two physical and two spiritual, that will help lead you to the point of surrender to God. The two physical disciplines are daily exercise and fasting. The two spiritual disciplines are spiritual reading (primarily with Scripture) and prayer. The meditations in this book will help guide you as you strive to put these disciplines into practice.

Don't be afraid when your weaknesses are brought to the surface. That's the entire goal of these disciplines. The words to keep in mind throughout our Lenten journey together are the ones that the Lord spoke to St. Paul: "My grace is sufficient for you, for my power is made perfect in weakness" (2 Corinthians 12:9). That weakness is actually a blessing: It will draw you closer to God. When you push yourself to what you think are your limits, you'll realize you have to rely on God to go any further.

On that note, let's hit the ground running, as St. Mark does in today's Scripture reading. In the first chapter of his Gospel, Mark gives us a brief introduction before jumping into the account of Jesus' baptism. In this very brief passage, Mark doesn't waste a single word. As the Spirit descends upon Jesus, the Father declares, "You are my beloved Son; with you I am well pleased" (Mark 1:11).

What we see declared at Jesus' baptism is, in a hidden, sacramental way, what God declares at our own baptism. As the *Catechism of the Catholic Church* (CCC) tells us, Baptism makes us "'a new creature,' an adopted son of God, who has become a 'partaker of the divine nature,' member of Christ and coheir with him, and a temple of the Holy Spirit" (CCC 1265). In other words, just as the Father is speaking these things to Jesus at his baptism, he also speaks them to *you*. At the moment in Baptism when you become his adopted son or daughter, God makes this declaration of love to you.

Many Catholics don't fully get this, myself included. They just don't live it. They read this Scripture passage and think that the Father is just speaking to Jesus rather than to us. But in reality, this is the message that God is constantly trying to tell you: You are his child. You are his beloved. And he delights in you.

This is where our Lenten journey starts. Everything from this point on is about accepting these truths. The goal is to simply believe, internalize, and live these truths, removing every obstacle to them in your heart and mind.

That's where surrender comes into play. We can accept these truths with our whole hearts, knowing that because God loves us so deeply, he will work everything out for our good. God is always pouring out a waterfall of love and grace upon us as he did at our baptism; all we need to do from this point on is to surrender to it.

## Respond

Look up a Catholic prayer of surrender or trust: for example, the *Suscipe* prayer by St. Ignatius; the "Prayer of Abandonment" by St. Charles de Foucauld; the "Surrender Novena" by Servant of God Don Dolindo Ruotolo; or the "Litany of Trust" by the Sisters of Life. Which line (or lines) of the prayer(s) do you most struggle with? Journal about these lines or bring them into conversation with God.

_____

_____

_____

_____

_____

_____

_____

_____

# Repent

*Read Mark 1:12–28*

*"The time is fulfilled, and the kingdom of God is at hand; repent, and believe in the gospel."*

## Reflect

St. Mark tells us that after Jesus' baptism, right after the Father spoke from heaven and called Jesus his beloved Son, "the Spirit immediately drove him out into the wilderness. And he was in the wilderness forty days, tempted by Satan; and he was with the wild beasts; and the angels ministered to him" (Mark 1:12–13). Even though Jesus was tempted by the Devil and dwelled among wild beasts, God still took care of his needs. Through his time in the desert, Jesus shows us that we can have confidence in God because even in times of trial, temptation, and hardship, he will provide for us. Even when we struggle with our Lenten disciplines and sacrifices, he is ready to minister to us and share the grace we need to see them through.

Before we can do that, though, we need to repent of our past sins and bad habits. *Metanoia*, a Greek word which we use for "repentance," literally means "a change of mind." After Jesus leaves the desert and begins his public ministry, he urges his listeners to "repent, and believe in the gospel" (Mark 1:15)—in other words, to turn from their past ways and allow their minds and hearts to be changed. When we repent, *really* repent, we should feel genuine sorrow for our sins. We should be saddened by the knowledge of our sins, but that grief is necessary so that we can fully receive the Gospel, the Good News.

Without genuine contrition, real sorrow for our sins, any outward gestures of repentance we make will be empty. Fasting, almsgiving, and other forms of penance are good in themselves, but if they are not motivated by a real change of heart, they will be empty, and we will continue to fall repeatedly into the same sins. We'll make no spiritual progress; we will simply go through the motions without *moving* anywhere. Another Lent will come and go, leaving no lasting impact upon our lives. Our repentance, our sorrow for sin, is transformative; since we have the hope of salvation through Christ, we can allow that sorrow to spur us to continually turn towards him and grow closer to him.

St. Mark notes that as Jesus begins his preaching, he calls Simon Peter and Andrew to follow him. His call requires a dramatic change of mind; they left behind all they knew, "left their nets and followed him" (Mark 1:18). From St. Luke's account, we also know that Simon fell at the feet of Jesus, saying, "Depart from me, for I am a sinful man, O Lord" (Luke 5:8). Simon does not believe he is worthy of the call, but it is precisely this recognition of his own sinfulness that prepares him to accept Christ's invitation. Jesus tells Simon, "Do not be afraid" (Luke 5:10); as Simon turns from his old ways and allows his mind to be transformed, he knows that some new way is necessary. Simon is ready to accept that new way Christ has planned for him—to become, together with his brother Andew and the other disciples, "fishers of men" (Mark 1:17)—even if he doesn't fully understand it yet.

Repentance does not imply a one-time event. *Metanoia* involves turning to God again and again. As we know, Peter does not live sin-free the rest of his life after being called by Christ; on the contrary, he will betray Jesus three times during the events of the Passion. Allowing God to change our minds and transform our hearts means we are called to an ongoing process of deeper conversion, a process that continues for the rest of our lives. In undertaking this work, we must be driven and determined, receptive to the promptings of the Holy Spirit.

As we journey on through Lent, let's ask for the grace to "change our mind" and repent. Moments of temptation and struggle are ahead; let's trust that the Lord will provide for us through these moments. And if ever we don't feel like we are up for the task, like Simon Peter, let's take Jesus' words to heart: "Do not be afraid" (Luke 5:10).

### Respond

When we recognize our wrongdoing and see our sin for what it is, we sometimes fall into the trap of despair. We trick ourselves into thinking that we can never overcome our sins or bad habits. What is one such sin with which you've fallen into this pattern of thought, and how can you gently correct yourself to overcome the habit? Ask God to protect your mind against despair and encourage you with the gift of hope.

# Healing

*Read Mark 1:29–45*

*"Moved with pity, he stretched out his hand and touched him, and said to him, 'I will; be clean.'"*

## Reflect

As Jesus moves through Galilee—preaching, healing the sick, and casting out demons—it's remarkable how incredibly dynamic he is. He works tirelessly for the sake of the Kingdom of God. The verses from Mark 1 that we read today give us a snapshot portrait of Jesus' public ministry: He is a man of action and authority, and everyone around him recognizes that fact—so much so that multitudes come straight to his door (see Mark 1:33).

Yet as much as Christ pours himself into his work in service of others, he also demonstrates the importance of prayer. Jesus strikes this perfect balance between the interior life and a life of action. He heals many, but he takes time to pray alone: "And in the morning, a great while before day, he rose and went out to a lonely place, and there he prayed" (Mark 1:35). Such moments of intimate conversation with the Father did not happen without intentionality; his fame made it almost impossible to find some alone time during the day, so Jesus had to rise early and seek out a deserted place. He purposefully makes time and shows us that as important as it is to be in relationship with others, our relationship with God cannot take a backseat.

Fostering our relationship with God requires stillness and silence. Even if we fill our time with many good things, the things we're called to do in service to others—feed the hungry, clothe the naked, visit the sick or imprisoned, comfort the dying and grieving—if we do those things without spending time with God, we will fall into the trap of busyness, not holiness. We'll start to cling to our role as God's servants, ignoring God's offer of friendship. As a result, we try endlessly giving, and we forget how to receive, drawing from an empty store. Our growth in holiness and the spiritual life can only take place if we take time to be with God, separate from any other kind of activity, so that we can truly listen to him.

Something else we learn from these verses in Mark's Gospel is how much God desires our healing. When a leper comes to Jesus, seeking to be healed, he says in faith, "If you will, you can make me clean" (Mark 1:40). Per Levitical Law, those who suffered from leprosy in Jesus' day were cast out from society, shunned and avoided for their condition. We can almost hear the hesitance in the leper's statement: *I know you can heal me—but will you do it?* In response, Jesus does not reject the leper; instead, Mark tells us that he is "moved with pity," and he tells the leper, "I will; be clean" (Mark 1:41). We can almost hear Jesus saying, *Of course I will do this for you!* The moment Jesus speaks these words and touches the leper, the disease leaves him.

If we gaze at the mental portrait of Jesus which this passage paints for us, we see someone worthy of our trust. God does not shun us; he is not appalled by our brokenness, wounds, addictions, or weaknesses. He is always reaching out to us with a love that longs to touch our hearts so that we may be "made clean." He longs to see us well and able to live in joyful communion with him, the life for which we were created.

Therefore, we can surrender to him in trust. He not only has the power to heal us, but he deeply desires to heal us, too. He understands our pain. He knows our suffering, and he wants our healing even more than we do. We can find no better person in whom to place our trust and ask for healing.

## Respond

What is a particular ache you've been feeling within yourself, something for which you seek healing? Pray or journal about his compassion for your suffering and his desire for you to be "made clean" and be well.

_____

_____

_____

_____

_____

_____

_____

_____

_____

_____

_____

_____

_____

_____

_____

# Belonging

*Read Mark 2:1–12*

*"When Jesus saw their faith, he said to the paralytic, 'Child, your sins are forgiven.'"*

## Reflect

In yesterday's reflection, we looked at Jesus' healing of the leper. As we talked about before, lepers were outcasts, isolated from the larger community. When Jesus touched the leper to heal him, he was not simply banishing the physical disease from the leper's body; he was also welcoming the leper back into a larger social and spiritual community.

One of the most fundamental desires in every human heart is for belonging. We want to know our part in the story, how we fit into the picture, where we belong in the group—and we want others to appreciate our presence there as well. God placed this desire for belonging in us: He created the human heart, and this desire for belonging ultimately pulls us towards him.

In today's passage from Mark's Gospel, we see another person who is seeking healing and belonging: a paralytic. But it is not just the paralytic; there are four other men, the paralytic's friends, who help bring the paralytic to Jesus so that he can be healed. In this passage, we see the creativity of love and the power of holy community. When they can't get to Jesus in a straightforward way, this group climbs onto the top of the house he's in, breaks a hole in the roof, and lowers their friend down on a mat! Genuine love finds a way, at all costs. If these men were willing to go to such lengths on behalf of a member of their community, what obstacles are we willing to break through to get to our Lord? How much work are we willing to do to be healed? What are we willing to do for the sake of another person's healing?

When Jesus sees the paralytic, he doesn't respond in the way we may at first expect. Instead of healing the paralytic physically, he looks into the man's heart and calls him "child," or in some translations, "my son" (Mark 2:5). He draws the paralytic into relationship with him, showing him that he is loved, before declaring that his sins are forgiven. In this, Jesus rightly orders the needs of the soul alongside the needs of the body. While physical health and healing are important, our human soul is of inestimable value—and our spiritual healing should take priority.

That said, God does not care for the spirit and forget about the body. After giving the paralytic spiritual healing through forgiving his sins, Jesus tells him to "Rise, take up your pallet and go home" (Mark 2:11)—and the paralytic immediately obeys, his body healed. God sees us in our physical need *and* our spiritual need; he cares for both. When either our physical health or spiritual health is neglected, our whole person suffers. Jesus longs to heal us in body and in soul.

For this reason, in order to make this Lent fruitful, we will strive to engage our heart, mind, body, and soul in loving the Lord. To this end, we have our four spiritual disciplines: spiritual reading, prayer, fasting, and physical exercise. As we journey deeper into this Lent, we need to prepare ourselves to be stretched, to be challenged, and to grow both physically and spiritually—because both, body and soul, are vital for our growth in holiness.

## Respond

Who is someone in your life who may need some help in coming to the Lord or in developing a deeper relationship with Jesus? In love for both this person and for the Lord, be creative in thinking of ways in which you can bring the love of Christ to this person.

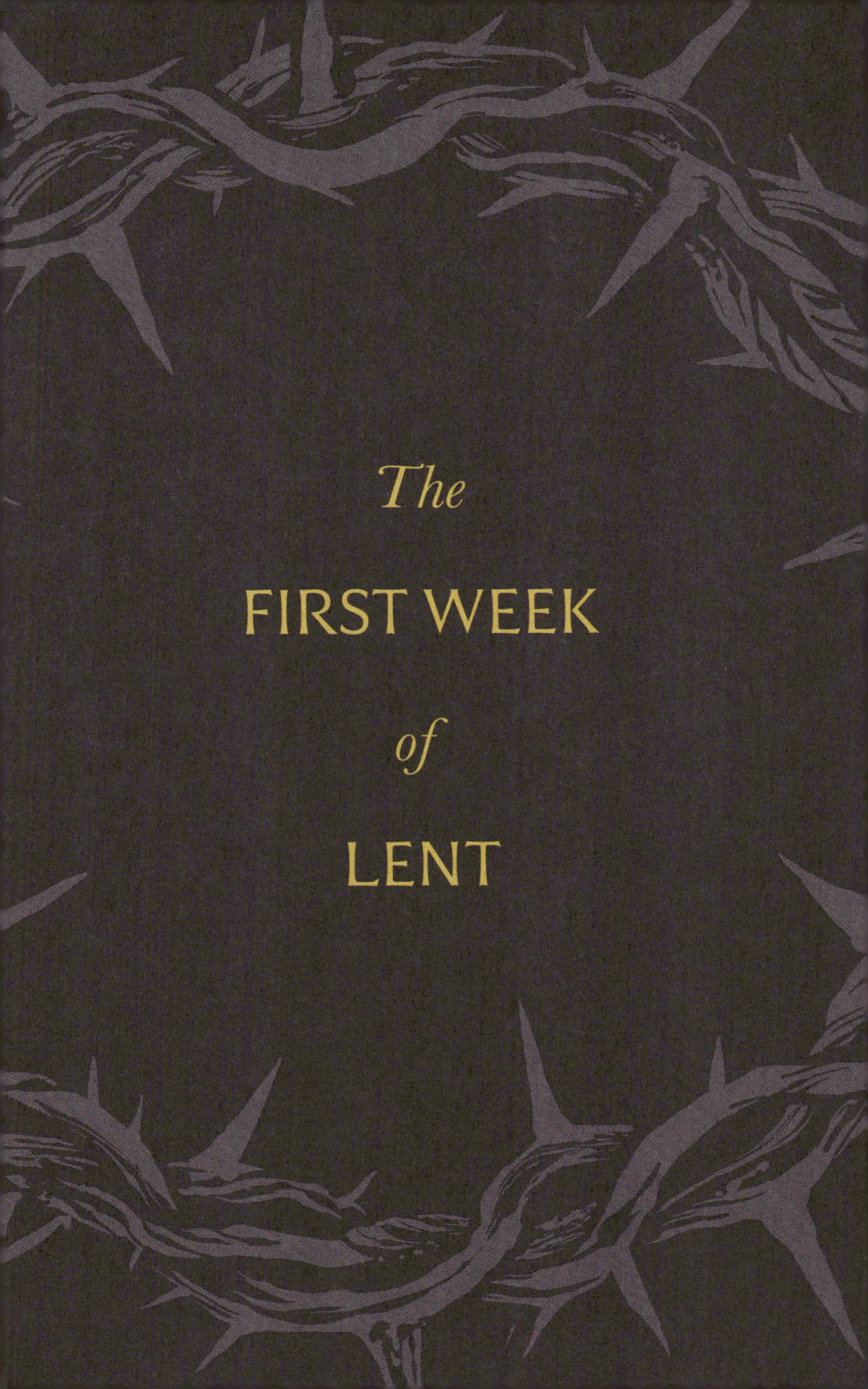

# The

# FIRST WEEK

## of

# LENT

### The First Week of Lent

As we enter into this first Sunday of Lent, we must prepare. Sometimes it is difficult to figure out what we want to "give up" for the Lenten season. Satan will often tempt us during this time, making us feel alone. But the Lord is calling us to a greater purpose and to walk alongside him through temptation.

The Lord gives us our identity and our purpose in life. The Devil will try to twist our identity so that we begin to question ourselves as sons and daughters of God. It is tempting to act like someone else, especially when we're trying to fit in—but God wants us to be who he made us to be, to act like Jesus did while he was being tempted by the Devil. Although we might have moments when we feel unsure about what to do, we need to call on the Lord and ask for his guidance. Let's bring God more into our everyday lives so that we may trust in who we are and the identity that he has given us!

## Challenge of the Week

Write a list of the things you are going to work on throughout Lent. Place this list somewhere you can see and remember every day. For younger children, you can create a "Lent bingo" that you place on the refrigerator and mark items off whenever a Lenten "task" is completed (such as praying a Hail Mary once a day, going to Eucharistic Adoration, or going to confession).

## Prayer of the Week

Lord, help guide us and reveal to us our identity that is defined by you. Reveal to us your divine nature and instill in us the trueness of your word. This Lent, help us to remain steady in ourselves and to ward off temptations, staying steadfast to your will. Amen.

## Bible Verse

"But he answered, 'It is written, "Man shall not live by bread alone, but by every word that proceeds from the mouth of God"'" (Matthew 4:4).

## Song of the Week

**"40 Days"** (Matt Maher)

# Identity

*Read Genesis 2:7–9; 3:1–7; Romans 5:12–19;
Matthew 4:1–11*

*"For as by one man's disobedience many
were made sinners, so by one man's
obedience many will be made righteous."*

## Reflect

From the beginning, one of Satan's most devious strategies to pull us away from God has been to attack our identity. We see this with Adam and Eve in the story of the Fall. The Serpent directly contradicts God, saying, "You will not die" (Genesis 3:4)—and he implies that Adam and Eve are really meant to be gods in their own right, on their own terms. In this, the Serpent sows a subtle seed of doubt in their minds, making them question God and their own role as God's beloved creation, made in his image and likeness. Satan attacks their relationship with God, too, claiming that God is actually working *against* them and holding them back from realizing their true potential. Adam and Eve listen to the Serpent, and the outcome is disastrous.

Centuries later, Satan tries using the same strategy when he tempts Jesus in the desert. We talked about Jesus' temptation in the desert briefly last week: After Jesus is baptized and the Father anoints him with the Holy Spirit, calling Jesus his "beloved Son," he goes to the desert to be tempted by the Devil.

In the wilderness, Satan tries to strike at Jesus' very identity: "If you are the Son of God, command that these stones become loaves of bread"; "If you are the Son of God, throw yourself down" (Matthew 4:3, 6). Notice that intentional word: *If.* The Enemy loves to convince us that our identity is rooted in our performance: "If you're really X, prove it and do Y." Satan tries to convince Jesus that *if* he's really God's beloved Son, he should do whatever he pleases. *If* he is God's son, he should prove it.

In the face of the Enemy's attacks, Jesus shows us what to do. Against every attack, Jesus replies with humility and the Word of God. He never doubts his identity as the Father's beloved Son, for he trusts the words that his Father spoke to him—and he deflects Satan's attacks with the words of Scripture. By keeping himself anchored in the truth of God's Word, Jesus is able to reply with humility and trust, believing that God would provide and that he didn't have to prove himself or grasp for anything himself. In the moment of temptation, the Holy Spirit supplied Christ with the words needed to counter the Enemy's attacks. He waits to supply us with the same defense if only we rely on him rather than on our own resources.

As we're getting established in this Lenten journey, let's check ourselves and make sure that we're not trying to build a name for ourselves or craft an identity rooted in mere performance, as if trying to prove that we are God's beloved sons and daughters. Instead, let's take this opportunity to reaffirm our identity as sons and daughters in Christ. Through whatever wilderness this Lent takes us, let's reflect with awe and gratitude on the words of St. John and take them to heart: "See what love the Father has given us, that we should be called children of God; and so we are" (1 John 3:1).

## Respond

Spend some time meditating on Romans 8:14–17. What words most strike you in this passage? In what respect do you feel like your identity as God's son or daughter is being challenged or attacked? In what way do you feel like your dignity as an heir of God is not being recognized? Try to identify the particular lie being spoken to you about your identity in these attacks so that you can reject that lie with the knowledge of who you are in Christ.

# Attention

### Read Mark 2:13–28

*"As he passed on, he saw Levi the son of Alphaeus sitting at the tax office, and he said to him, 'Follow me.' And he rose and followed him."*

### Reflect

There is a common trap we sometimes fall into in our spiritual lives: We stop watching to see how God is at work. Perhaps it's because we get distracted or caught up in the busyness of our daily routines. Perhaps it's because we've forgotten how to pay attention. Perhaps it's because we think we already know what God is going to do, and we think, *Sure, God can do all things—just not in my life.*

But just because we haven't been watching doesn't mean God hasn't been working. It's like when you've been staring at something, but then you start to zone out and your vision begins to blur. When we "zone out" in our spiritual life, we struggle to see our relationship with God clearly. In the meantime, even when our vision is blurry, God is continually at work. He has been moving dynamically in all parts of our lives; we've just lost sight of him. He tells us, "Behold, I make all things new" (Revelation 21:5)—but in our own failure to behold, we can't recognize the newness of his work. And when we fail to see, we miss opportunities to respond to his grace.

To avoid this trap, we should attend to the Lord with the alertness of Levi (also called Matthew). In today's passage from Mark's Gospel, Levi immediately gets up and follows Christ as soon as he's called. The beautiful result we see immediately afterward is that because Levi pays attention and responds to Jesus' call, others like him—sinners and fellow tax collectors—are able to encounter Jesus at Levi's house. His attentiveness, by extension, blesses other people around him.

Even the Pharisees and scribes seem to hang on Jesus' words more attentively than we do. That said, we shouldn't follow their example. The religious leaders constantly watch and listen to what Jesus does and says, but it isn't to learn from him or follow him. Instead, they challenge him and question his behavior. While the religious leaders constantly watch and listen in order to find something to use to attack, we should instead be constantly watching and listening in order to follow, like Levi.

If we want to pay closer attention to Jesus, we can start by attending more closely to his work within our own hearts. When you're doing your spiritual reading, pay attention to the movement of your heart. If something strikes you, don't ignore the feeling—stop and connect with God! He notices all the movements of our hearts. If they are not beneath his notice, we should not give them any less attention. He is knocking at the doors of our hearts, waiting for us to hear him.

As an example of paying attention in this way, here's one way to do an Ignatian meditation on the scene of the meal at Levi's house. Put yourself in the scene. First, picture the judgmental gaze of the Pharisees falling upon you. Imagine being one of the disciples they accost with the question: "Why does he eat with tax collectors and sinners?" (Mark 2:16).

Consider what happens next as Jesus hears the question and answers the Pharisees. Imagine the gaze of Jesus falling on you as he says, "Those who are well have no need of a physician, but those who are sick; I came not to call the righteous but sinners" (Mark 2:17). What emotions does this bring up? What do you think Christ is trying to tell you through this response?

Remember that God often speaks to us through the still, small voice, a whisper in our hearts. It can show you corners of your heart that you never knew existed.

## Respond

What is one area of your life in which you've been waiting for God to step in and make new? How do you think he's been using this period of inactivity to bring about a different change than the kind you've been expecting?

_____

_____

_____

_____

_____

_____

_____

_____

_____

_____

_____

_____

# Strengthen

*Read Mark 3:1–19*

*"He appointed twelve, to be with him, and to be sent out to preach and have authority to cast out demons."*

## Reflect

Recently, during a time when I felt I was falling apart in every sense of the term (physically, emotionally, spiritually), one of my spiritual advisors told me, "Just surrender it to God, and tell Jesus exactly how you're feeling. If you feel like a mess, tell him. If all you have to give him is a mess, give it to him."

I'm sure that many of us would respond to that suggestion just as I was tempted to in that moment: "Well, I don't think he wants *that.*" But in truth, he *does.* He doesn't want us only at our best—he wants us in our mess, too.

If you want proof, consider who Jesus chose for his twelve apostles. The Twelve were a bit of a mess. St. Mark gives us a glimpse of this in our reading for today. The sons of Zebedee, James and John, were called the "sons of thunder" for their hotheadedness (Mark 3:17). Judas Iscariot goes on to betray Jesus later. Even the head of the apostles, Simon Peter, denies Jesus three times and makes plenty of mistakes well before then. They squabble over who is the greatest, misunderstand Jesus repeatedly, and get caught up thinking of earthly concerns. Yet Jesus calls them anyway, knowing all that is going to happen, knowing very well their mess.

But looking at the messiness of the Twelve gives us *hope*, doesn't it? Through them, we see that we are not disqualified by our failings—that even in our brokenness, we can still follow Christ. Christ did not call the Twelve because he was looking for the perfect servants. He didn't choose them because they were the best candidates for the job of spreading the Gospel. He chose them, above all, "to be with him" (Mark 3:14). He is seeking communion and family. He calls us out of nothing other than pure love.

Jesus doesn't just work on us while we remain idle. He wants to enter our brokenness, to heal us *with us*. He incorporates us into his work of healing, asking us to move toward him. Earlier in today's passage from Mark, Jesus could have cured the man with the withered hand no matter where he was, with no action on the man's part. Instead, he tells the man, "Stretch out your hand" (Mark 3:5). He views the human person holistically, knowing that in this physical movement is a movement of the heart as well. In this small movement is an openness, a vulnerability, and a surrender. The man makes his weakness more visible to all, revealing his desire for healing, and surrenders to whatever Jesus has in mind for him.

In a letter to her sister, St. Thérèse of Lisieux wrote, "Do not let your weakness make you unhappy. When, in the morning, we feel no courage or strength for the practice of virtue, it is really a grace: it is the time to '*lay the axe to the root of the tree*,' relying upon Jesus alone."[1] St. Thérèse was herself no stranger to feeling dismay at her own weakness, and yet she is able to encourage her sister because of the comfort she herself found in radical surrender.

In moments of particular weakness, we are given the grace to see more clearly that we can do nothing without God. Our own weakness doesn't matter; he is the one in control, and what limited strength we have is from him anyway. In this knowledge, we are liberated to focus our efforts on surrendering entirely to him and encouraging others to find the same comfort. We can do as St. Thérèse does—and as Jesus does literally in today's reading—and "strengthen the hands that are feeble" (Isaiah 35:3 NAB).

## Respond

Being a follower of Christ often means doing hard things, sometimes things we would much rather not do. Sometimes it can seem tedious trying to work out regularly, but we know that taking care of our bodies follows naturally from spiritual discipline—and working out shows good stewardship of the gift of health that God has given us. Today, as a spiritual practice (rather than to lose weight or get in shape, though that may be a bonus), devote some time to physical activity, offering your effort up to the Lord.

# Recognition

*Read Mark 3:20–35*

*"How can Satan cast out Satan? If a kingdom is divided against itself, that kingdom cannot stand."*

### Reflect

Skeptics of Christianity like to paint Jesus as simply a human teacher, on the same level as someone like Socrates, Buddha, or Boethius. They say Jesus was one among many other great moral thinkers, but unfortunately, his teaching was just too ahead of his time—and, ultimately, he was killed for it.

The one troublesome detail that messes up this "moral teacher" theory is Jesus' claim to be God. If he really were a great moral teacher, but nothing more—*not* God—then he was a liar, intentionally deceiving others toward some personal gain. But it doesn't seem plausible that anyone who is lying for gain would be willing to die such a horrible death, all for the sake of a lie. Was Jesus crazy, then? Well, from his teaching, we see no evidence of insanity.

C.S. Lewis popularized this point through what he called the "trilemma": Jesus was either (1) a lunatic, (2) a liar, or (3) the Christ. In *Mere Christianity,* Lewis explains, "A man who was merely a man and said the sort of things Jesus said would not be a great moral teacher. He would either be a lunatic—on the level with the man who says he is a poached egg—or else he would be the Devil of Hell. You must make your choice. Either this man was, and is, the Son of God: or else a madman or something worse."[2]

The trilemma ultimately points to a more relatable question: Why do we struggle so much to acknowledge that Jesus is Lord? Even those of us who are Christian, who profess that he is the Lord, sometimes struggle with actually allowing him to rule over our lives.

We see in today's passage from Mark's Gospel that the religious leaders also struggled to accept that Jesus was the Son of God. As Jesus says in today's reading, if he really were the Devil casting out demons, the scribes and Pharisees would have no reason to be so cross with him. In fact, they should have been rejoicing at Satan's downfall: "If Satan has risen up against himself and is divided, he cannot stand, but is coming to an end" (Mark 3:26). (It's interesting that in this same chapter of Mark, we see that the actual demons recognize Jesus as the Son of God—and they are none too pleased with Christ's work.)

A little further in this passage, as Jesus talks about blasphemy against the Holy Spirit, he warns us not to attribute to Satan the works of the Holy Spirit. In doing so, we call evil that which is good, and vice versa. It is to call the works of God bad, to deny the goodness of the work God is trying to do within our own lives.

These passages are like a mirror: We can use them to help us pause and consider whether we actually trust in Jesus' claims as much as we think we do. Are we really willing to let Jesus be Lord of everything? Jesus encourages us to invite the Holy Spirit into our hearts, to welcome his work in our lives. The reward is incredibly vast: to become part of Jesus' family. We allow God's Word to be brought to birth in us; we share that Word with others and do the will of the Father as Christ's brothers and sisters.

As you face the question of whether Jesus is Lord of your life, I encourage you to allow his reign within your own life. There is no other king who offers so great a reward to those in his service.

## Respond

Today, undertake a dietary fast (within reasonable limits). The goal is to feel the "ouch"—not to hurt ourselves, but to learn to offer sacrifice. When you do feel the "ouch," turn your thoughts away from food and toward Jesus; tell him you are hungry for him.

# Listen

*Read Mark 4:1–20*

*"The sower sows the word. ... Those that were sown upon the good soil are the ones who hear the word and accept it and bear fruit."*

## Reflect

God communicates in stereo. Stereo sound is played through multiple channels at once, which creates the effect that you're surrounded by the sound. When God tells us something, he will often communicate it via multiple "channels" and confirm it in various ways. He speaks to us through his holy Word, through different actions and events, and through the people in our lives, his faithful ones. Knowing this, we need to be aware of the different ways in which God can speak to us and to learn to listen attentively.

One way we're intentionally encountering God this Lent is through a personal examen—a form of daily prayer where we think through our day and consider the times we felt close to God, along with the moments where we struggled to stay close to him. With an examen, before you look over your day, it's important to ask the Holy Spirit to guide you and help you listen to how he is speaking. Pay attention to your reactions, common themes, or repeated nudges from the Spirit—and if something keeps coming to mind, take note of it.

Christ's parable of the sower is so important because it spells out how to follow God's will and live as a member of Jesus' family. In this parable, he not only tells us to listen well but gives us clear instructions for how to do so. First, we must hear (or read) God's Word. But it's not enough to hear it; we have to understand it, fully grasp it, or else it will fall on the path and be snatched away. Sometimes that means if we don't understand something right away, we should turn to other trusted sources to help us learn. If we can't explain something in our own words, it means the idea hasn't yet sunk in. We need to delve further into it so that it can sink deeper into us.

Second, we need to pray with Scripture and connect with God. Sink your roots into his Word and let reflecting on Scripture truly become part of your daily routine. Otherwise, although reading the Bible might produce some small changes at first, they won't last—and his Word won't be able to become your source of daily nourishment or encouragement. Eventually, you'll give up trying to read and understand it.

Finally, we must respond with action. If we don't actually respond to the Word, taking it to heart and answering its call to action, other alternatives will outgrow God in our lives. The weeds of worldly concerns will sprout up and choke the Word within us. We are never stationary; we are always moving either closer to God or further away. We are always producing some kind of fruit, whether good or bad. If God's Word is not allowed to grow within us, something else will take its place.

When we think of what it means to be a good listener, we probably imagine someone simply being silent and attentive. Jesus tells us that listening well is more than that. He tells us that listening well to God's Word involves three steps: hear the Word, accept it, and bear fruit. God's Word is not content to sit idle. It *lives* within those who receive it, driving them to action. The letter to the Hebrews tells us, "For the word of God is living and active, sharper than any two-edged sword, piercing to the division of soul and spirit, of joints and marrow, and discerning the thoughts and intentions of the heart" (Hebrews 4:12). Receive God's Word, and when it calls you to action, respond to it. Let it live in you.

## Respond

In what concrete way might God be calling you to act on his Word today? Rather than thinking of a grand gesture, think of a little thing in your daily life that God may be asking you to do differently.

# Asleep

*Read Mark 4:21–41*

*"The wind ceased, and there was a great calm. He said to them, 'Why are you afraid? Have you no faith?'"*

## Reflect

The cry of the disciples in the midst of the storm is one of the most common prayers each of us says throughout our lives: "Teacher, do you not care if we perish?" (Mark 4:38). The book of Psalms asks the same questions: "How long, O Lord? Will you forget me for ever? / How long will you hide your face from me? / How long must I bear pain in my soul, / and have sorrow in my heart all the day?" (Psalm 13:1–2).

In our darkest moments, this is the simple, anguished cry of our hearts: *Lord, do you not care?* With the storm clouding our sight, how can we see God's hand at work? How can we understand those moments when it seems that God is sleeping while we're suffering?

In the face of such moments, St. Thérèse of Lisieux gives us a surprising alternative. She said that in times of trial, she would let Jesus go on sleeping in the boat! In a moment of great spiritual aridity, Thérèse said, "Jesus was sleeping as usual in my little boat; ah! I see very well how rarely souls allow Him to sleep peacefully within them."[3] Perhaps you're thinking, "Well, I am no St. Thérèse. I think I'll just wake up Jesus."

Jesus wants us to turn to him in our need, of course—and he also wants us to trust him. When we ask him, "Lord, don't you care about me?", he responds with a question of his own: "Why are you afraid? Have you no faith?" (Mark 4:40). In other words, "Don't you know who I am? Don't you trust me?"

Jesus juxtaposes fear with faith. Fear is ultimately the result of our attempt to play God and control things that are well beyond our control. But faith comes from our choice to recognize that only God is God—and we can let him take control with the confidence that he's not going to let us down.

Notice how quickly the twelve apostles panic, even though Jesus is right there beside them. Even after seeing all the great works he's done so far, they still succumb to the fear that Jesus is going to let them drown! Their eyes are on the storm, not on him. As easy as it is for us to dwell on the storms we're currently facing, we instead need to keep our eyes on *him*, to trust *him*, to imitate *him*. We need to rest in his love and trust that if he's sleeping in the boat, it is because he knows that all will be well. He can see beyond the storm, even if we can't.

A great indicator of our growth in the spiritual life is where we are on the spectrum between fear and faith. We can't be in both states at the same time. We can either cry out to the Lord as waves of fear wash over us, or we can fix our eyes on the Light that shines in the darkness. He remains with us in the boat and never abandons us. In sleeping, he only shows that we need not fear.

## Respond

Many of us are worriers; worry is a form of fear. It's not the same as identifying a problem and taking it to God in fervent petition. If you catch yourself worrying today, use it as a reminder to make an act of faith in Jesus. Instead of accusing him of not caring, tell him you're afraid and then surrender the situation to him. Whenever you catch yourself in such moments, pray the line from the "Surrender Novena": "Jesus, I surrender myself to you, take care of everything."

# Follow

*Read Mark 5:1–20*

*"Go home to your friends, and tell them how much the Lord has done for you, and how he has had mercy on you."*

## Reflect

In today's Scripture passage, Jesus and his disciples come to the country of the Gerasenes, a region right on the border of Gentile territory. They soon encounter the demoniac who is living among the tombs.

Among the many stories of Jesus casting out unclean spirits, this one stands out for several reasons. For one, we see a man who very vividly represents spiritual death through sin: He lives among the tombs, away from his hometown, and he has been physically chained, representing his spiritual bondage to sin. He harms both himself and others, and the best efforts of his fellow men are to try to subdue him rather than free him. Christ, on the other hand, isn't looking to restrain him: He's looking to restore him to the fullness of himself. For two, when the demoniac sees Jesus, he immediately rushes over and begins to worship him—and the demons inside the man acknowledge his identity: "What have you to do with me, Jesus, Son of the Most High God?" (Mark 5:7). Even the demons recognize Jesus for who he is. Finally, even though Jesus heals one of their own, the people of that region don't rejoice in the miracle; instead, they are afraid. In fact, they beg Jesus to leave! Their hearts are closed off, and they don't want the radical change Jesus would bring into their lives.

Perhaps the most interesting part of this story is how Jesus responds to the man after he is no longer possessed. After he is freed from the demons, the man begs Jesus to let him stay with him and follow him, and Jesus refuses. You may be thinking, *Hold on. I thought the whole point was that we're supposed to follow Jesus—and now, just when he has someone who really wants to do that, he says no?* What's going on here? Is God just a contrarian? Does he toy with us and give us X when we ask for Y?

Not at all. Instead, I think the key lies in this man's request. It is the key to Jesus' heart: The man *wants* to be with him. This man has the heart of a disciple, and so Jesus tells him to proclaim the Lord to his family and friends. He sends the man out to be an active disciple in his hometown. The man surrenders to God's will and obeys Jesus' instructions: He immediately begins to proclaim God's goodness, and his words soon bear fruit.

This is a wonderful illustration of a close relationship with Jesus. Closeness isn't about physical proximity; it's about accepting the Father's will and carrying it out. In so doing, we are members of his family. Jesus subverts this man's expectations (and ours) by expanding the idea of what it means to follow him. Because the man obeys, God is able to work through him dynamically. This man gets to be a follower of Jesus not because he travels around with him, but because he is doing God's will and sharing the Good News with those in his community. He follows him in the very act of walking the other way.

This is a powerful lesson for all of us. Jesus doesn't call us to stay physically close to him inside the walls of our parish.

Instead, he asks us to remain with him as we go out into the world, sharing the Gospel with our community. In saying yes to Jesus and accepting that mission, we are able to touch the hearts of others, to bring the light of Christ to those who do not know him or who have formerly rejected him.

## Respond

Make a list of some of the things you're most grateful for this week. How do you think God is trying to work through those things in your life? What is he particularly trying to say to you with these specific blessings?

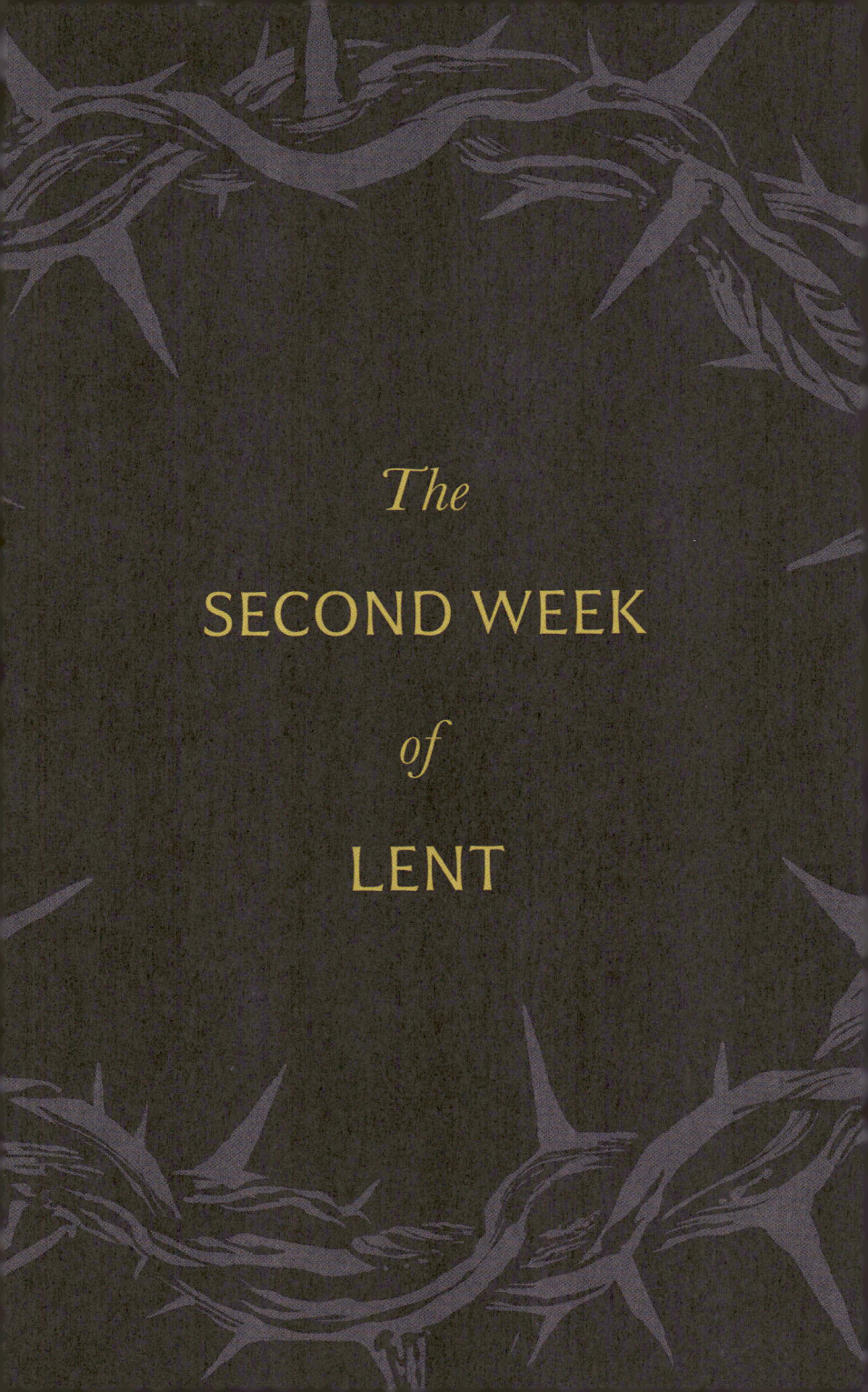

# The

# SECOND WEEK

## of

# LENT

## The Second Week of Lent

Do you remember your baptism? Many people are very young—just babies!—when they are baptized. During our baptism, the priest poured water over our heads and blessed us with sacred chrism oil, sealing us with the gifts of the Holy Spirit and cleansing us of our sin. When Christ was baptized, the Lord revealed something important to us about him: Christ's divine nature. Both at Jesus' baptism and later at the Transfiguration, God revealed that Christ is his beloved Son and part of the Holy Trinity. This special moment encourages us to recognize the significance of the Sacrament of Baptism, particularly our own baptism. Through Baptism, God invites us into this same union of the Trinity so that we may actively live with his divine grace and be members of his family.

Through our baptism, we are given our identity in Christ. We become God's beloved sons and daughters, and we are called to follow him. Although it is sometimes difficult, God gives us the tools to help us through challenging times. With prayer, we are able to draw ourselves closer to him and ask for his guidance. Let's spend time in prayer this week and thank God for our baptism and new life in him!

## Challenge of the Week

This week, reflect on the Sunday Gospel reading (Matthew 17:1–9). Consider how God is calling you to look at the Transfiguration. Either draw or write down your thoughts and share them when you're gathered for dinner or before a nighttime prayer.

## Prayer of the Week

Lord, help us to renew our baptismal vows with you so that we may come to better know and understand your endless love for us. Help guide us during this time of Lent so that we may remain in union with your will. Instill in us the importance of our identities as your beloved sons and daughters. We ask this through your guidance. Amen.

## Bible Verse

"He was still speaking, when behold, a bright cloud overshadowed them, and a voice from the cloud said, 'This is my beloved Son, with whom I am well pleased; listen to him.' When the disciples heard this, they fell on their faces, and were filled with awe. But Jesus came and touched them, saying, 'Rise, and have no fear'" (Matthew 17:5–7).

## Song of the Week

**"Lord, Who Throughout these Forty Days"** (Claudia Frances Hernaman)

# Reminder

*Read Genesis 12:1–4a; 2 Timothy 1:8b–10;
Matthew 17:1–9*

*"A voice from the cloud said, 'This is my
beloved Son, with whom I am well pleased;
listen to him.'"*

## Reflect

I'd love to be a saint—a real, honest-to-goodness friend of Jesus. I'd love to be able to say that he really and truly is first in my heart and above everything else in my life. I'd love to be able to say that I put him before all else. The truth is, I can't say that—not yet. But today's Sunday Mass readings give us help and hope for pursuing an ever-deepening relationship with God.

In today's Gospel reading from Matthew, we once again have a revelation of the Trinity: we have the bright cloud of the Spirit coming over the Son and the voice of the Father declaring the truth about Jesus' identity: "This is my beloved Son, with whom I am well pleased" (Matthew 17:5). Jesus is the beloved Son; he is the Father's chosen one. The Father is pleased with him and delights in him. God speaks these words for our sake, for the sake of those who so often forget the truth. What the Father says to Jesus, he also says to you: You are his beloved! You are his precious child, made in his image. God really, truly delights in you.

This message is precisely the same one we explored earlier on Ash Wednesday—yet so often, we need to hear again the same truths that we already know for them to truly sink in. We need someone to remind us about who Jesus is because *he* is the one who reminds us of who *we* are. It is all too easy to forget who we are in relation to God. We forget that God really, truly loves us—not for anything we've done, but simply because of who we are: his! When you need reminding, turn to this moment of Jesus' transfiguration and hear the Father's words as if he is speaking to you: *You are my beloved son. You are my beloved daughter. With you I am well pleased.*

In a sense, all the grace in our lives springs from the grace of our baptism. All our sanctification and growth come from living out and believing the truths of our baptism, because in that sacrament, we became adopted sons and daughters of God. The rest of our lives should be guided by that knowledge, that new identity in him.

During the Transfiguration, there is one extra bit to what the Father says: "Listen to him" (Matthew 17:5). This is not a confirmation of who Jesus is but a command for the rest of us. Listen to Jesus, God's Word, and you will remain grounded in the truth of who you are. As Jesus' friends, we can imitate him by turning to God in prayer and recalling that he is present with us. To do this, to listen to Jesus' words, is to be a contemplative. In time, he will lead us higher up the mountain, but for now, just sit with these truths. Soak in your identity as beloved son or daughter. Engage your imagination with this, imagining the Father speaking these words to you and about you. At the conclusion of your prayer, hold fast to this knowledge of your God-given identity, and listen to the words of Christ: "Rise, and have no fear" (Matthew 17:7).

Think of the three elements of Christ's identity that the Father declares to each of us. He declares that you belong to him as his son or daughter; that you are beloved; and that he takes pleasure in you. Which of these truths do you most have trouble accepting or contemplating? What wounds does that speak to that still need healing in you?

_____

_____

_____

_____

_____

_____

_____

_____

_____

_____

_____

_____

_____

_____

_____

_____

_____

_____

_____

_____

# Faith

*Read Mark 5:21–43*

*"He said to her, 'Daughter, your faith has made you well; go in peace, and be healed of your disease.'"*

## Reflect

In today's Scripture passage, we have two examples of faith. First, we have a woman suffering from hemorrhages for twelve years. Second, we have Jairus, whose daughter is about to die. Both teach us something about the nature of faith. In this new Israel, Jesus' new family, our relationship with him is based on faith, on really trusting him because we know him from our heart. As we read this passage, we need to ask ourselves: How is Jesus teaching us about faith, whether privately lived or publicly expressed—and how is he stretching us?

Let's look at our first example with the woman who suffered for twelve years. She believes that she has but to touch Jesus' clothes and she will be healed. Her great faith enables her to receive healing through Jesus' power. But then Jesus calls upon her great private faith to go public. Now there's a scary thought: giving public testimony before such a large crowd. The woman probably found it just as scary as we do. She could have just kept quiet and hid within the crowd; however, she comes forward, fearful and trembling, and she falls down before Jesus in front of everyone, declaring what happened to her. Her faith is rewarded. Because of her response, the woman is physically cured and spiritually reassured: Jesus tells her, "Daughter, your faith has made you well; go in peace" (Mark 5:34).

In our second example, Jesus again juxtaposes fear and faith, just as he did with the apostles in the midst of the storm. Even as Jairus receives the most devastating news that his daughter has died, Jesus seems absurdly calm: "Do not fear, only believe" (Mark 5:36). It's not about never feeling fear; this would be impossible. It's about making a choice not to remain in fear. We don't focus on our problems—we focus on God instead. There's an old saying: "Don't tell God how big your problems are. Tell your problems how big God is." Jairus receives the most dreadful words a parent can hear, and yet when Jesus says she is only sleeping, Jairus believes him. He stays the course, following Jesus—and in the end, his daughter is brought to life again.

In the face of two extreme forms of suffering, long physical ailment and profound grief, Jesus gives us an answer that seems ridiculously simple: "Do not fear, only believe" (Mark 5:36). Our mistake, though, is often in thinking that our extremely complicated problems need extremely complicated solutions. Fear wants to convince us of this, to persuade us that our problems are too complex to ever be solved. Jesus pushes back against this and tells us that we don't need to worry about puzzling everything out. Instead, like the woman and Jairus, we just need to have faith and trust in him to take care of it.

## Respond

How does your faith need to grow? In going more public, in overcoming the fear of what others might think? In believing more in what God can do for you? We should strive to achieve the level of faith shown in today's passage: the simple, childlike trust that believes in the midst of the deepest suffering, Jesus' touch is all that is needed to cure us.

# Resilience

*Read Mark 6:1–13*

*"He charged them to take nothing for their journey except a staff; no bread, no bag, no money in their belts."*

## Reflect

We have two distinct events in today's passage: Jesus' rejection at Nazareth, followed by the mission of the Twelve. It's wonderful to read the Gospel in this way, to see these events connected to one another as part of a flowing narrative. Sometimes when we encounter these readings in Mass, we forget that these passages aren't just stand-alone vignettes. They're actually interconnected, and as we see the greater context of the Gospel narrative, we get to see what passages the Holy Spirit lines up for us.

For example, in the second part of today's passage, we have the twelve apostles being sent out to evangelize for the first time. This must have been glorious, exciting, challenging, and also slightly terrifying. If I had been there, I would have been so afraid of rejection. But here is the wisdom of these Gospel events. To set up this second part of the passage, we first have the account of Jesus being rejected in his hometown.

In the first part of Mark 6, Jesus goes ahead of his apostles to show them the way. He wants to prepare them for the challenge ahead, to show them that they don't need to be afraid—so he goes someplace where he is guaranteed to face rejection. As he says, "A prophet is not without honor, except in his own country, and among his own kin, and in his own house" (Mark 6:4). He knows exactly what he's doing: He shows them they don't need to be disheartened by rejection. When a town doesn't welcome them, they simply need to shake the dust of that town from their feet and move forward. In all this, Jesus gives the apostles an example of work that doesn't seem to bear any immediate outward fruit.

How good Jesus is! He understands our fears, and he wants to help us overcome them, especially our fear of sharing the Gospel with others. He is a teacher who walks the walk, who braves all the trials we could face to show us that we don't need to be afraid of them.

When we see people doing difficult things, we tend to put them in a different category from ourselves, telling ourselves that they're an entirely different type of person, uniquely equipped to deal with those difficulties. The apostles set out with basically nothing for the journey to preach a new and challenging message, and they were tasked with casting out demons and healing the sick. Looking at their mission, our immediate reaction is probably, "I would never have had the strength to do that." But the apostles had never done anything like this before, either. God gives us the strength we need when we need it; God goes before us to show us the way.

## Respond

Today, we are once again going to focus on exercise as a spiritual discipline. One of the greatest obstacles I experience with working out is when I feel like I can't do it, though in fact I just don't want to do it. God did an amazing thing when he made our bodies, and yours is a wonder! The truth is your body can probably do way more than you've ever done with it. As St. Paul says, "Glorify God in your body" (1 Corinthians 6:20). He may not have been thinking of your particular Lenten workout discipline, but it still applies. Use your workout today to push yourself a little bit, to glorify God by marveling at the incredible things he enabled you to do.

# Dying

### Read Mark 6:14–29

*"Some said, 'John the Baptist has been raised from the dead; that is why these powers are at work in him.'"*

### Reflect

Today's story continues yesterday's theme of rejection. Yesterday, we explored Jesus' rejection at Nazareth before the Twelve were sent out to preach the Gospel to the surrounding region. Today, we see John the Baptist experiencing the ultimate form of rejection in his imprisonment and unjust death.

This is not an easy Scripture passage to digest. Just the thought of it is difficult to contemplate. It forces us to ask ourselves what we would do in the same situation. Would you be willing to pay that price? If your love were put to the test in that way, would it see you through? Ask yourself: *How real is my discipleship? Am I really all in, like St. John? At what point do I tap out with my faith?*

These are uncomfortable questions. When considering the answer, I find it helpful if you ask yourself if you'd be willing to die for someone else you love: spouse, kids, parents, friends. If we can say yes to that (or even just "maybe"), we should be aiming for a love for God that is at least this real, at least this deep.

I'm afraid my weakness and fear would betray me. But this fear can be a powerful motivation: It can drive us to ask our Lord to give us more courage, to help us surrender our fear that such a dramatic thing could be asked of us. As Jesus tells us during his agony in the Garden of Gethsemane, "Watch and pray that you may not enter into temptation" (Matthew 26:41). We also pray for grace to abandon ourselves fully to God's will—such that if we are ever tested in that way, we will respond with courage as John the Baptist did, as Christ himself did.

We probably won't be asked to pay this price in this way, but we certainly will be asked to die to ourselves and to our fear of rejection. It is in this daily practice of dying to self in little ways that we gradually build up the strength to die to self in a more drastic way.

What we see in the description of John the Baptist's martyrdom is how many opportunities Herod and Herodias had to die to themselves—and yet they chose to ignore them. Herod arrests John because he can't bear to hear someone criticize his sinful actions. Herodias harbors a grudge against John, refusing to forgive him and entertaining the desire for another's harm. Without any thought to her daughter's benefit, Herodias also takes what could have been a gift to her daughter and makes it into an opportunity to satiate her desire for vengeance. Herod makes a rash promise and, in his pride, refuses to humiliate himself in front of his guests by going back on his word. Their choice to ignore these opportunities for selflessness or humility not only means that they don't die to self, but they also take the life of an innocent man.

Let's avoid the example of Herod and Herodias and follow the example of John the Baptist. Let's practice dying to ourselves each day, in little ways, learning to die in another's place through small acts of self-sacrifice. Let's learn to say to God and to others, "Not my will, but yours, be done" (Luke 22:42).

## Respond

One of my greatest obstacles to fasting is my fears: my fear of growing prideful, of discomfort, of becoming uncharitable, of collapsing with weakness, of getting sick, of what people will think, etc. Jesus spoke of fasting as a basic need of the spiritual life, and the Church does, too. First, talk to Jesus and engage your mind. Ask what *he* wants for you, not what your fear wants. If you're still freaking out, then maybe talk to someone (a priest, a doctor, or a faithful friend) who has experience with fasting.

# Reliance

*Read Mark 6:30–44*

*"Taking the five loaves and the two fish he looked up to heaven, and blessed, and broke the loaves, and gave them to the disciples to set before the people."*

## Reflect

When you are going on a trip, what is the number-one thing you take with you? Beyond keys and clothes, what's your most important item? Oftentimes, it's the credit card. It gives us a sense of security and comfort. We think, *Even if I forget something or lose something, everything will be fine. I can always buy what I need. Visa, I trust in you.*

This is nothing new. The apostles had their own versions of comfort and security—and yet Jesus sends them out for their mission with almost nothing: no food, no money, no spare tunic (see Mark 6:8–9). He does so not to decrease the amount they have, but to increase their trust. He's trying to teach them to rely entirely on God, without having a backup plan.

If we are part of God's family now by faith, by hearing and obeying God, then we need to keep growing in trust. This is where the rubber meets the road in our faith. Otherwise, we'll be continually crying out, "Lord, Lord!"—but we'll really be worshipping our bank account, our job security, our abilities, our reputation, or some other idol that we rely on for comfort. Let's put our money where our mouth is and learn what it truly means to rely on God, not just to believe that God will work through our various idols in order to help us. God doesn't need our resources to help us; the world doesn't need what we can give from our own supply, either. God only needs our faith, our surrender to him—and the world needs what the Father can supply through us. To let him be seen, we need to surrender our self-reliance and rely completely on God.

What we see in today's reading is that we don't need to persuade God to have compassion for us in our trials. St. Mark tells us that immediately after Jesus got off the boat and saw the crowd, "he had compassion on them, because they were like sheep without a shepherd" (Mark 6:34). They didn't need to convince Jesus to notice them in their poverty. His heart was stirred for them from the start. He saw their need for him; he saw that they felt lost, confused, and directionless. And so he fed them—spiritually through his teaching and physically through the miraculous multiplication of the loaves.

Even those closest to Jesus feel as though they have nothing to offer. Tired and hungry from their mission trip, they give to Jesus from their very emptiness and hand over what little they have left. It must have been a wrench watching the Lord take the loaves and fish. They were probably thinking, *Just when we finish our mission of pouring ourselves out for others, just when we finally have a bit of time to ourselves with the Lord, this entire multitude shows up. Just when we finally have a little bit of food of our own, we have to hand even that over.* But if they hadn't handed over that little bit that they had, they and all who were with them would not have experienced the sheer abundance that followed. Through our act of surrendering a little, the Lord gives us everything we need and more.

## Respond

What is something you recently had to surrender control of and hand over to the Lord in faith? Ask him to fill you in the midst of this loss and to help you give to him openhandedly.

_____

_____

_____

_____

_____

_____

_____

_____

_____

_____

_____

_____

_____

_____

_____

_____

_____

_____

_____

_____

_____

_____

_____

_____

# Courage

*Read Mark 6:45–56*

*"They all saw him, and were terrified. But immediately he spoke to them and said, 'Take heart, it is I; have no fear.'"*

### Reflect

It was a dark and stormy night. The apostles were out on the boat, struggling through a squall so strong that it was enough to frighten even these fishermen who were well used to navigating the storm-tossed Sea of Galilee. For most of the night, they fought against the wind and the waves.

Where is Jesus at this point in the story? He isn't in the boat this time: He's waiting. He doesn't come to them until the fourth watch of the night, which in modern terms would be somewhere between 3:00 and 6:00 in the morning. You may be thinking, *Well, that seems rather cruel.* But it really depends on our conception of God. Do we presume that God is loving or unloving? Is our immediate assumption that he's doing this for our ultimate good, or do we jump to the conclusion that he's just making sport of our misery?

During these trials, these storms in our lives, God often waits and lets us struggle for a while, but it's not to be cruel. It's because these moments make us recognize our own powerlessness and give us a chance to recognize our own need—a need that only God can fulfill. In these situations, which are so entirely beyond our control, our hearts are more receptive to God.

But these situations don't just serve to emphasize our weakness; they also help us grow in courage and strength. Jesus is training his disciples, and part of that training involves letting them try their hands at difficult things. He doesn't abandon them; he's watching them and praying for them all the while.

They say chicks who don't get to break themselves out of their own eggs don't survive; they need the extreme workout in order to be able to survive outside the egg. Growth is just as vital as birth. Without the opportunity to try things and make mistakes, we will be left stunted.

This is the second time we've seen the apostles facing a terrifying storm. This time, Jesus comes walking towards them on the water and terrifies them even more. Jesus addresses them in their fear a second time: "Take heart; it is I; have no fear" (Mark 6:50). That "heart," that courage, is not the absence of fear. Courage is simply choosing to trust God in spite of fear. Jesus asks us to recognize him in the storm, to trust that he has everything under control. After encountering him there, after abandoning ourselves to his will, we are able to face the storm calmly.

Sometimes the terrifying thing is that God's hand *is* there, and we're worried about what he will do. This isn't the attitude of love, though; love requires trust in the beloved. We don't have trust in God because he always makes everything easy and delightful for us. We have trust in him because we know that even if we can't understand the reason for the storm, we know that he is only letting us struggle through it because it will ultimately be better for us than having no storms at all.

## Respond

Abandonment to God's will is never comfortably achieved. You would think it would be easy, letting him take care of everything and not having to worry about it—yet we have to struggle and wrestle with our own will to let him take that load off our shoulders. Look up St. Charles de Foucauld's "Prayer of Abandonment" and focus on uniting your will with the will of the Father in an echo of Christ's words on the Cross: "Father, into your hands I commit my spirit!" (Luke 23:46).

# Discipline

*Read Mark 7:1–23*

*"He said to them, 'You have a fine way of rejecting the commandment of God, in order to keep your tradition!'"*

## Reflect

I would have hated to be on the receiving end of Jesus' condemnations. *So* uncomfortable! But Jesus isn't worried about being nice and comforting all the time. He came not to bring peace but a sword. He's not afraid of shaking things up when we need it or of challenging us to our core.

If our immediate reaction to passages like today's is one of relief, we should take a moment to consider why that is. We can read the questions of the Pharisees and think to ourselves, *Oh, those silly Pharisees—how can they not just see the goodness of what Jesus is doing?* But if that's our way of thinking, we ought to pause and ask why we're so quick to assume that we're not just like the Pharisees.

The truth is, Jesus *does* speak sternly to us sometimes, mainly because we doubt his methods as the Pharisees did. We also fail to see the goodness of what he's doing in our lives. We all fall into the trap of just going through the motions, growing quite contented with ourselves for having so many daily prayers and disciplines, even when they're not done with love, when our hearts are far from him.

Is Jesus condemning all disciplines in this passage? No, but he does say that they need to lead us closer to God and make us more like him rather than less. Empty spiritual practices don't just have a neutral effect; they can lead us into self-complacency and sometimes cause us to look down upon others as we marvel at our "extreme piety."

Take our Lenten disciplines, for example. We can do them badly, or even sinfully, if it's all just a big ego trip for us. Or they also turn sinful if we're just being hypocritical, seeming to be holy while in fact our hearts are opposed to God at every turn. In those cases, Jesus says the same thing to us as he said to the Pharisees: "You have a fine way of rejecting the commandment of God, in order to keep your tradition!" (Mark 7:9).

This is why we have to take a look at our fruit, what comes from within us. What is coming out of you as you do your daily Lenten disciplines? If it's a bit ugly, that's actually good! That doesn't mean you're bearing bad fruit; it means you're being purified and spiritually stretched. Did you "hit the wall" this week? Did you reach a place where you didn't think you could do it anymore? If so, that means you've reached the place where you actually feel your need for God. The goal is not to break you but to help you grow.

Some people hit the wall by feeling unable to do fasting or other disciplines, but some hit the wall by feeling their inability not to get prideful at their spiritual accomplishments. Either one can be used to grow in humility. To hit the wall is to really feel the "ouch" deeply. Just turn to God and admit that you need him to the point of deep yearning. What a blessing to be able to actually feel this, to know that your heart has not grown lukewarm!

Failure is actually essential for true victory to come to us by his power. If you are weak, then you qualify as one of those who will receive God's help. Remember how St. Paul said, "When I am weak, then I am strong" (2 Corinthians 12:10)? Don't be discouraged, then, if your fasting or other disciplines are bringing certain shortcomings to the surface. This is an opportunity to notice them and bring them to God, asking for his strength to overcome them. Blessed are they who hit the wall!

## Respond

Take a look back over your week. In what sense did you hit the wall this week in your disciplines? Did you do much comparing of yourself to others? Did it make you feel proud or ashamed? Do you think you are doing well or badly with your disciplines? Whatever the answers are, the way to profit from them is to turn them to God and surrender them to him, resolving to do better next week.

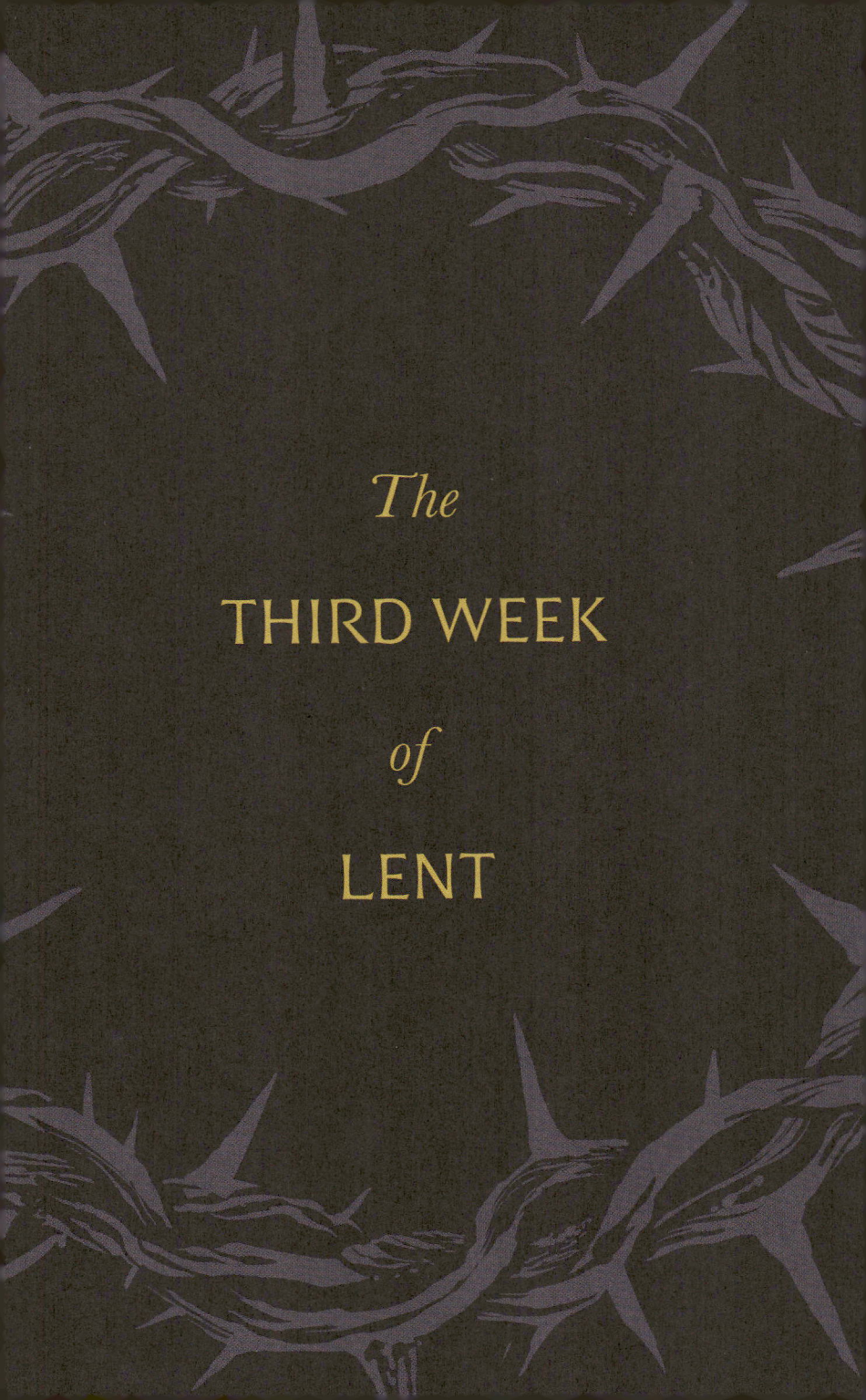

*The*

# THIRD WEEK

*of*

# LENT

## The Third Week of Lent

Have you ever felt rejected? Maybe you didn't make the varsity team or didn't get picked first for a gym-class game. In these moments, we often feel as though no one wants us or that we aren't "good enough." But God calls us to a deeper truth: We are desired by God! In the Gospel story about the woman at the well, we meet a Samaritan woman who is rejected because of her current living situation. Even though she is rejected, Christ comes to her in this moment, seeking her out and making her feel seen. Jesus saw all of her hurts, desires, and rejections, and he took that upon himself so that she could accept the Good News and share it with others.

God sees you. He calls *you*. Christ is constantly chasing us in love. He sees us at our worst moments, and he still desires us and wants what's best for us. By giving us the gift of the sacraments, Jesus reminds us that we are called to be pursuers—disciples—of Christ. Our ultimate goal and destination in life is heaven, and to obtain that goal, we need to direct ourselves toward Jesus every day through our prayer and our actions.

## Challenge of the Week

Offer your chores up to God. Chores can sometimes be seen as a nuisance and frustrating, but before you begin each chore, offer a small prayer to God to redirect your thoughts.

## Prayer of the Week

Oh God, you call us even when we sin. You seek us out in our moments of rejection and feelings of destitution. Help guide us out of these times of darkness and help us to see our worth that is defined by you. Reveal to us the beauty of the sacraments and instill in us the importance of your will. We ask this in your name, Our Lord, Jesus Christ. Amen.

## Bible Verse

"Jesus said to her, 'Every one who drinks of this water will thirst again, but whoever drinks of the water that I shall give him will never thirst; the water that I shall give him will become in him a spring of water welling up to eternal life'" (John 4:13–14).

## Song of the Week

**"Lord, I Need You"** (Matt Maher)

# Pursued

*Read Exodus 17:3–7; Romans 5:1–2, 5–8; John 4:5–42*

*"Every one who drinks of this water will thirst again, but whoever drinks of the water that I shall give him will never thirst."*

### Reflect

In today's Sunday Gospel reading, Jesus is like a treasure hunter. He's seeking out a different kind of treasure, though, something of inestimable value—but it's not something many people would consider precious.

In John 4, Jesus goes to Samaria and encounters his treasure: the woman at the well. The woman is an unlikely treasure for several reasons. For one, she is a Samaritan; the Samaritans and the Jews did not get along. For two, John tells us that the woman is fetching water at noon, in the heat of the day—a detail that tells us that she is rejected by society. Instead of collecting water in the cool of the morning along with the other women of the area, this woman goes later, all alone. She may be ostracized because of her multiple divorces and current living situation. By all appearances, she is avoided and rejected by everyone. The apostles are amazed that Jesus is even speaking with her.

Yet Jesus does not reject or avoid this woman. In fact, he *pursues* her. Even though Jesus is tired from his journey, he's not too tired to seek her out. He speaks to her at length, one on one. Few people in the Gospels ever received such a privilege—namely, to be singled out like this and evangelized personally by Jesus. Of all the people Jesus encounters during his public ministry, he chooses to tell this Samaritan woman who he is: He's the Messiah.

The Samaritan woman desires something that we all desire: to be seen, and deeper than that, to be understood. This particular woman, though, has a profound thirst for both these things because she has experienced such a deep lack of them in her life. Jesus responds to the extremity of this need by filling it with an equally extreme outpouring of understanding, more than the woman could ever have imagined. He shows her that he sees her heart, knows her entire history, and pursues her all the same. He gives her this devoted attention—not in spite of her sins, but because of them. The Samaritan woman had been drawing from the same old well for quite some time, living in the same patterns of sin and always ending up thirsting again. After Jesus enters her life, how rapidly we see her welling up with living water!

When the woman returns to the town, she goes from being pursued to being a pursuer herself, to becoming an evangelist. She tells everyone in town what Jesus has done for her, and the townspeople not only see her but also *listen* to her and come to believe because of her (see John 4:39).

As you read this passage today, realize that *you* are being pursued. You are the object of God's desire. Jesus pursues you every day through prayer and the sacraments. In confession, Jesus pursues you to heal you and cleanse you from sin. In Holy Communion, he pursues you to dwell within you, body and soul. Through prayer and Scripture, he provokes, encourages, comforts, and challenges you to grow in holiness and bear fruit through how you live your life. Keep this in mind today: Jesus wants *you*.

## Respond

In prayer today, simply dwell in the knowledge that you are relentlessly pursued by Jesus. Thank him for the gift of that pursuit of your heart. Consider offering him this response: "Lord, help me to delight in the realization of being pursued by you. I long to see the signs of your love and desire for me. Grant me the grace to experience your pursuit of me through the sacraments, the world you have created, the friends and family you have given me, and the many gifts and graces you give me each day. Grant me the grace to pursue you in return, accepting the unique mission you have given to me. Amen."

# Humility

*Read Mark 7:24–37*

*"They were astonished beyond measure, saying, 'He has done all things well; he even makes the deaf hear and the mute speak.'"*

## Reflect

Across all four Gospels, Jesus encounters women, and through those encounters, they bear good fruit. Consider the Samaritan woman we reflected on yesterday. After her encounter with Jesus, she believed in him, reformed her life, and told all her neighbors the good news of the Messiah. Similarly, the Syrophoenician woman we read about in today's Scripture selection is quite spectacular.

In this account, the Syrophoenician woman pleads with Jesus on behalf of her daughter, who is possessed by a demon. The woman is bold and yet incredibly humble in expressing her need, which makes for a powerful, positive combination. When she comes before Jesus with her request, at first it seems like Jesus is telling her no. He says, "Let the children"—namely, the people of Israel—"first be fed, for it is not right to take the children's bread and throw it to the dogs"; in response, the woman says, "Yes, Lord; yet even the dogs under the table eat the children's crumbs" (Mark 7:27–28). This woman just keeps coming, taking Jesus' own metaphor a step further to present her request again.

In the end, Jesus tells her, "For this saying you may go your way; the demon has left your daughter" (Mark 7:29).

For some of us, this exchange with the Syrophoenician woman leaves us confused or a little uncomfortable. After all, Jesus could have simply healed the woman's daughter from the moment she made her request. He didn't need to have this back-and-forth about dogs and table scraps with the woman. So why did he do it? Why bother?

The answer is a lesson in humility. Some people would likely have been indignant with Jesus after making such an unflattering association with dogs, but this woman is different. We see her incredible humility in how she doesn't take offense at Jesus' words. Instead, she demonstrates great faith in Jesus—greater faith than many of the Jewish people—along with devoted love for her daughter. Her example teaches us that humility involves a "taking on" of sorts. The Syrophoenician woman receives Jesus' words and willingly "takes on" the place of someone outside of God's chosen people, yet still trusting Jesus' power and goodness. In a more profound way, Jesus "took on" our human nature at the Incarnation, coming down to our level to heal us and bring us back to himself. The woman's humility reflects Jesus' own humility—and for her humble faith, her daughter is freed from the demon.

How are we being asked to respond with the same humility and the same bold faith as the Syrophoenician woman? For starters, we can look at what we do when we don't like what the Bible says. When we encounter things in the Bible that we don't initially understand or like, our tendency is to step back from these passages and return to "safer" parables and stories that we know. Sometimes we want to step away from Scripture altogether. But while the stories we're familiar with are good, these places of complexity are a beautiful place to dive into this tension. I've always found that these difficult passages are the richest with hidden revelation. We have faith that we can 100 percent trust God's word, and we know that it is always good, so places of confusion can be occasions when we might be called to dive deeper into study, exploration, or prayer.

As you go through Lent, take these challenges to prayer, and sit in the tension, asking God to reveal his Word to you. Have a bold faith that he will resolve these tensions for you, and have humility in knowing that his thoughts are higher than your thoughts, but he can bring you to a better understanding.

## Respond

What's a Bible passage you've always found a little bit difficult, and why do you think you in particular struggle with it? Write it down and spend some time trying to understand what God is saying through this text. What jumps out at you, and what insights do you get from praying with these words?

# Trust

### Read Mark 8:1–21

*"I have compassion on the crowd, because they have been with me now three days, and have nothing to eat."*

## Reflect

The apostles' hard-heartedness and confusion in today's reading stand in amazing contrast to the woman in yesterday's reading. It's quite astounding. Even after the calming of the storm, even after all the miracles they have witnessed and healings they have seen, they still worry. These were the souls personally chosen by Jesus, and even their faith is so small.

In today's passage from Mark, Jesus shows that he is aware of the crowd's needs—and ours. He tells his apostles that he feels for the crowd because they have been with Jesus for days and don't have any food. "If I send them away hungry to their homes," Jesus says, "they will faint on the way; and some of them have come a long way" (Mark 8:3). In response, his disciples say, "How can one feed these men with bread here in the desert?" (Mark 8:4). In other words, they doubt: *How could we possibly feed this huge group way out here, in the middle of nowhere?*

Compared to the apostles here, we might be doing okay—or so we think, anyway, when we read these passages. But how often do we act just as the apostles did? How often do we receive great blessings from God yet still struggle to trust him? How often do we go from marveling at his power one moment to worrying and fretting in the next? We worry about problems similar to those Jesus has already solved for us in the past, even when he's right there beside us. After all this time, after all the things he's seen us through, why don't we trust him?

All of Jesus' miracles point to one reality: the goodness of God. With God, we don't have to worry. He is good. Even when the disciples ask, "How can one feed these men with bread here in the desert?" (Mark 8:4), Jesus doesn't chide them for their doubts. He doesn't grow impatient or frustrated with them. He simply asks them, "How many loaves have you?" (Mark 8:5). Jesus treats us the same way. His goodness isn't hampered by our mistakes or doubts or worries; all Jesus asks of us is to share with him what we have. Even if it doesn't seem like much, when we hand over what little we have to Jesus—our "lousy best," as Fr. Walter Ciszek would say[4]—he can take it and multiply it to satisfy all our needs.

It seems easier for us to remember suffering than to remember joy. Perhaps it's simply a matter of focus: it's so much easier to focus on the negative than it is to stay rooted in gratitude and remember our blessings. How quickly we forget the goodness of God! The apostles had already seen him multiply loaves and fish on a previous occasion (see Mark 6:34–44), but he does it again to remind them.

Let us remember: If Jesus looked after me yesterday, he'll look after me today. Was there ever a time in my life when I truly trusted him and he let me down? If he has been faithful and good before, then surely I can trust him to be faithful and good to me today.

## Respond

Something I both love and hate about doing exercise is that it is hard! This means I am very quickly confronted with my weakness of body and mind. Sometimes the toughest decision is simply to start and not give in to the thought that I don't have time for it today. Today is day 21, which is the magical number when some say a habit is formed, so if we've been faithfully doing our daily disciplines, then we may already have a habit formed or on the way. Let's focus on doing our exercise discipline today without waffling about it and asking whether or not we have the time. In your prayer, focus on doing the same in trusting Jesus; don't waver and overthink whether or not you should trust him. You know his heart is moved on your behalf, and you know his goodness. Reaffirm your trust in him.

# Belief

*Read Mark 8:22–30*

*"He asked them, 'But who do you say that I am?'"*

## Reflect

With today's reading, we reach the narrative midpoint in Mark. The halfway climax of the story is Peter's confession that Jesus is really the Messiah, the Son of God. This was not just St. Peter stating an opinion; it was an act of faith and required God's grace.

Jesus never told the Twelve directly that he was the Christ. He wanted them to come to that conclusion themselves. Through his actions, Jesus left a trail of breadcrumbs pointing to his identity as the Messiah—but his followers and the crowds had to pursue the trail and answer for themselves the crucial question: *Who is this man?*

This question is the most important question we will ever ask ourselves in this life. My mother asked me this question when I was a teenager, while I was lost in New Age beliefs and searching for truth. When my mother asked me, "Who do you say Jesus is?", my answer was very wishy-washy. Still, my mother didn't nag or react at all (except she probably prayed for me a lot after that). I didn't realize it at the time, but this question was an essential step in my journey back to Jesus. After I learned about him from the Gospels and St. Faustina's diary, I realized that the way I thought about him and the way he described himself were totally different.

Sometimes we gain our vision of faith bit by bit. As we saw in yesterday's reading, God's grace has been working steadily and gradually in the apostles' lives, removing their ignorance and doubt—until at last, St. Peter can confidently affirm Christ's identity. It's also like the man in the first verses of today's passage. Others tell the blind man about Christ, and they physically lead the man to him. But his healing takes place in stages. He gains partial sight back, but the way he sees things is warped. Then Jesus lays his hands on his eyes, and the man's sight is fully restored.

This reminds us that we need to be patient with those in earlier stages of their spiritual journey—and we need to be patient with ourselves as well. For us personally, we don't need to give others the entirety of everything we believe all at once. Sometimes it is enough to bring up the most important question—*Who do you believe Jesus is?*—and allow that question to open the opportunity for curiosity to grow and faith to take root. For our own sake especially, we shouldn't be irritated with ourselves if we've been working on growing in the same virtues for ages. We just need to keep working at them and keep letting God's Word take root in our hearts so that, little by little, our virtue will grow, and we'll be able to bear great fruit.

Today is a reminder to be patient and have trust that God can bring this work to bear fruit in yourself and in others. Just like the apostles, you have seen and heard much as we've journeyed with Jesus. Who do you say that he is?

## Respond

Picture yourself in the group of apostles as St. Peter makes his confession of faith. Perhaps think back to an occasion when you heard someone else making a similar public and confident expression of faith. What emotions does this bring up? Joy, gratitude, pride, jealousy, irritation? What does this say about your own faith and who Jesus is to you?

# Self-Denial

*Read Mark 8:31–38*

*"If any man would come after me, let him deny himself and take up his cross and follow me."*

## Reflect

The first Passion prediction must have come as such a shock to the apostles, especially right after St. Peter declares that Jesus is the Messiah. We see that, despite Peter having just made his big confession of faith, he still doesn't really understand how Jesus does things. He even takes Jesus aside and begins to rebuke him, the one he just affirmed to be the Messiah! In the course of a few verses, we see Peter go from being exalted among the apostles to being pretty harshly scolded: "Get behind me, Satan! For you are not on the side of God, but of men" (Mark 8:33). Yikes!

This is the great challenge we face in our faith: to surrender all our opinions about how God should do things. I have many such opinions about how I think God should operate—and they cause me a lot of suffering, actually. They ultimately are the ways I try to play God, though not very successfully. That's where so much of our suffering comes from: the clash between our will and God's. We try crafting this ideal situation in which we follow Jesus while we expect him to follow our will. But the Lord is very humble; he won't barge his way into my life. I have to open the door to him, to give him leave to actually be God and actually be Lord over me.

Jesus knew exactly how hard his words would hit when he said that anyone who wanted to follow him first had to take up their cross. Like a good physical therapist, Jesus finds where it hurts and pushes; that's how healing and growth come. In order to help us accept those words, he finds those things which we particularly don't want to give up—the areas in which we really don't want him to have control—and encourages us to release them for something better: namely, our healing. When he pushes on those areas, it hurts, and we often take that as a sign that God has withdrawn from us, but really, it's when he's calling us to come closer to him.

In her Nobel Prize acceptance speech, Mother Teresa said, "Love to be true has to hurt."[5] She told us to give to others not simply from our excess, but from a place of sacrifice, where it truly matters. The same goes for our love for God. Sometimes we try to give him the "excess" sacrifices; it's easy to make occasional sacrifices of things we only moderately like. But in order to really love God, we have to be willing to give even things we *really love* to him. When Jesus asks those things of us, it's because he's trying to push us to love more deeply, to help us stretch and grow in love of him.

Let's work then on listening to his voice when he asks us to give up our own ways and opinions. Let's try to think more as he does, even to the point of actually thanking him for sending us these crosses. When we accept the little crosses, we can see how much Jesus helps us carry them and how much they end up working for our good.

## Respond

How often do you "give 'til it hurts"? Do you give from your excess? Does your generosity toward others end whenever you're tired, angry, or sad? Or do you love even when it costs you? What can you do in your own moments of weakness or pain to keep loving others well, even in a small way? Find the times when you'd rather stay silent or avoid others and ask Jesus to "push" on those areas to help you give to someone when you'd rather hold back for yourself.

_____

_____

_____

_____

_____

_____

_____

_____

_____

_____

_____

_____

_____

_____

_____

_____

_____

_____

_____

_____

# Contemplation

### *Read Mark 9:1–13*

*"He was transfigured before them, and his garments became glistening, intensely white, as no fuller on earth could bleach them."*

### *Reflect*

Sometimes, Jesus calls us to come with him up the mountain, to join him in the stillness and silence of contemplation. Other times, he calls us to feed the crowds. We need a healthy balance of prayer and action in our lives. Both are good things, but sometimes even when we have a desire for a good thing (maybe preferring action and feeling unable to sit still), God asks us to turn from that thing to something else.

A perfect example of this tension between the contemplative and active lives is seen in St. John Vianney. In a time when many people in France had lost their faith in the wake of the French Revolution, God raised up a humble *curé*, a parish priest, who so devoutly tended his flock and ministered to others that he brought many, many souls back to living their faith. Even beyond his primary community in Ars, thousands from all over flocked to St. John Vianney to receive the Sacrament of Reconciliation. St. John Vianney often spent up to eighteen hours a day hearing confessions!

Knowing that, you could easily understand how St. John Vianney must have craved opportunities to spend time in silence and contemplation. He longed to retire and become a contemplative; he even left his parish in Ars at least once, but later he repented and returned! Like the three apostles on the mountain with Jesus, the *Curé d'Ars* had encountered the sweetness of contemplation, of connecting with God in a fulfilling and awe-inspiring way. And he understandably wanted to stay there—but while that would have been his preference, it apparently was not God's will for him. Not every good thing is God's will for us. Because of St. John Vianney's humble obedience and willingness to balance contemplation and action—to be a contemplative "in the world"—he ignited a love of the Faith in the hearts of his community and far beyond.

When we remain obedient to God's will in spite of our immediate desires and temporary feelings, God often uses our deeper longings to help us attain the greatest holiness possible, even if at the time we don't understand it. We should all strive to pray more in general, and the more we pray, the more we will want to pray—but when Jesus says to leave the mountain, we should leave. Surrendering our preferences, especially when it comes to doing good and holy things, is a tricky and delicate business. If the Devil can't get us via sin, he'll get us with holy activities that are not in keeping with our state in life. For instance, a father who goes to prayer meetings but in doing so actually neglects being present to his family is not acting as God would have him. His state in life is calling him to other duties.

This is why discernment is so vital. We need to seek out God's will, not just what feels good and holy in the moment. We need to not only have that balance of contemplation and action, but we need to have the humble obedience—like St. John Vianney—to acknowledge what God truly wants from us and surrender to his will. Only then can our obedience and surrender lead to greater blessings for ourselves and those around us.

## Respond

Are there any holy activities in your life that you would not be willing to give up if God asked them of you? Sometimes giving up those activities can feel like you're taking a step backward in your spiritual life. If you feel that way about one of those activities, what do you think that reveals about your idea of holiness? Does it mean you feel holiness depends on the number of activities or vocal prayers that you do? Does it mean you feel you have to earn God's love?

# Growth

*Read Mark 9:14–29*

*"All things are possible to him who believes."*

## Reflect

What is faith, really? Is it a guarantee that we can control God and get him to do tricks for us? No, of course not. That is magic: to control demons, sickness, nature, even other people. Seeking to be in control is the opposite of faith. Control is the warped version of the obedience that comes from faith.

With faith, we can do great things; as our Lord said, "Truly, I say to you, if you have faith as a grain of mustard seed, you will say to this mountain, 'Move from here to there,' and it will move; and nothing will be impossible to you" (Matthew 17:20). A lot of times, though, we get caught up in what our faith *should* enable us to do. We think, *Okay, Lord—I have at least a tiny bit of faith. Why isn't all this great stuff happening for me? You promised I could move mulberry trees and mountains if I just believed in you a little!* But on the other side of the coin is our own obedience to God that should come through faith. Through our faith, we are obedient to him—and so he makes things obedient to himself, through us.

Faith is about relationship, in encountering the other and letting them be themselves, especially God. It enables us to know that God can do all things, but it also lets God be God. It asks and then trusts. Our trust is in the fact that no matter what the outcomes are to our requests, he is always good, and he is always in control.

This is what prayer and fasting teach us. They *don't* teach us, "Do this and you'll get what you wish for"; rather, they teach us how to abandon all thoughts of controlling God and to depend on him entirely to bring about what is good and best for everyone.

Notice how both parties seeking this favor from God in today's Gospel have a problem of faith. The father doubts in Jesus' power—and meanwhile, the disciples believe too much in their own power. After all this time of following the Lord, despite having been taught to pray, the disciples still haven't fully grasped the purpose of prayer, the "surrender" aspect of it. By that point, they probably thought they had seen enough of how Jesus worked and thought they had the situation under control. That was exactly the problem.

It must have been difficult to hear Jesus tell them that this kind of demon can only be driven out through prayer. *Ouch.* They were probably thinking that they pray all the time, that they continually talk with our Lord. We often think the same thing: *I've been saying all these prayers and doing all these spiritual disciplines—so why isn't anything changing?*

More than adding a bunch of prayers to our daily routine, we, like the disciples, still need to grow in faith and in obedience to God. The plea of the boy's father is a very simple, earnest one and must have been very touching to the heart of our Lord: "I believe; help my unbelief!" (Mark 9:24). This is the tension we always struggle with: We believe, and yet we need God's help even to do that.

In *The Imitation of Christ*, Thomas à Kempis writes that Christ says to us, "Is there something too hard for me? Or am I like one of those people who says he is going to do something but then does not do it? Where is your faith? Hold fast and persevere. Be a man of boldness and great endurance. Consolation will come to you at the right time. Wait for me. Wait. I will come and care for you."[6] If you're struggling with your faith, don't fret. Just work on letting the mustard seed grow, on trusting him more, and surrendering your control.

## Respond

As we look over this last week, think about this matter of letting God be God. For me, I ask myself if I am overly attached to a particular outcome that I'm praying for or working towards. Is it possible that God has a better plan that I can't even imagine? He is always good, and as my youth leader years ago used to say, "God's best is best for everyone." Note any outcomes you're attached to, and then say a prayer surrendering them to him.

_____

_____

_____

_____

_____

_____

_____

_____

_____

_____

_____

_____

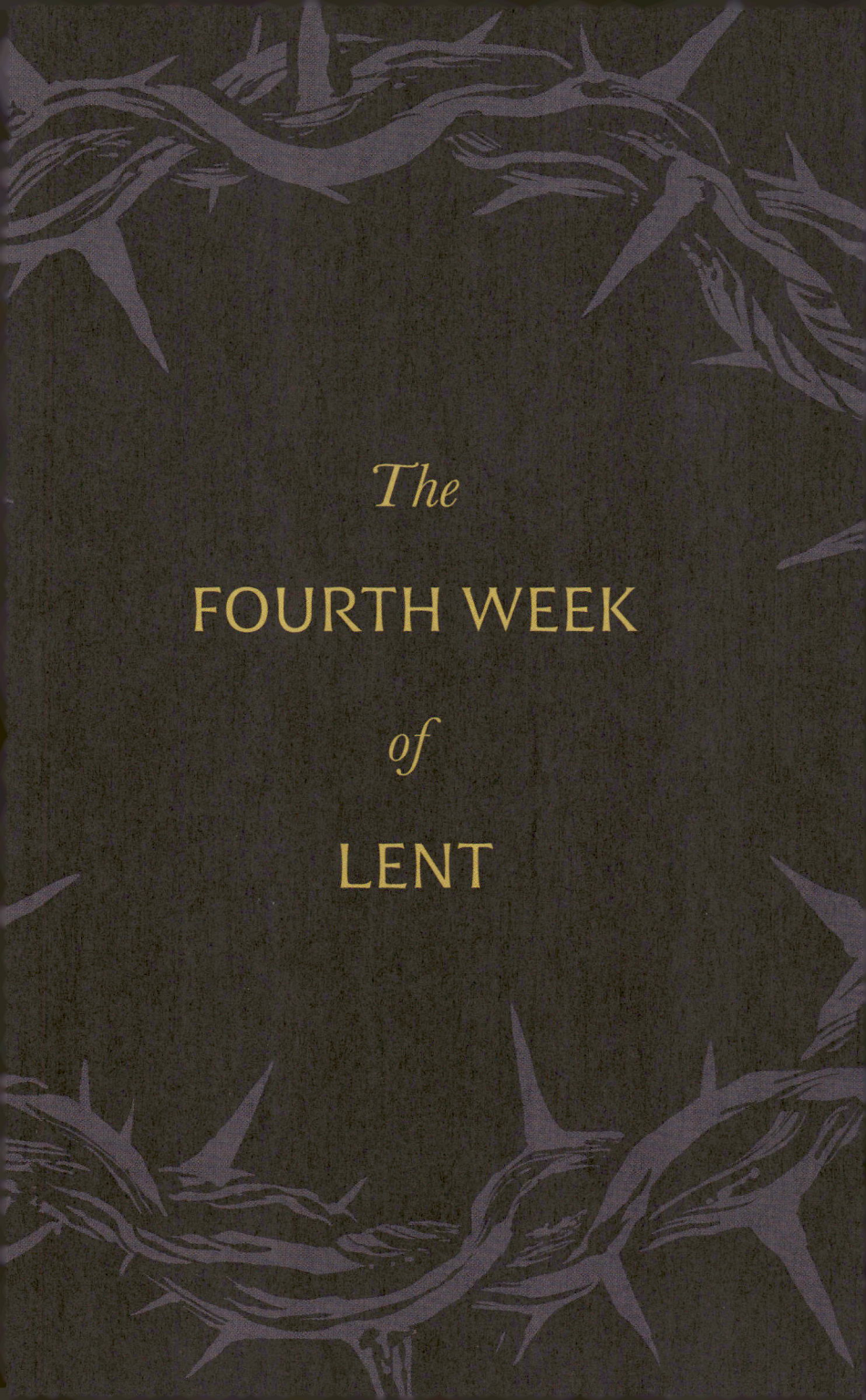

# The

# FOURTH WEEK

# of

# LENT

## The Fourth Week of Lent

Have you ever been outside or in your bedroom when it's really dark? As you stare out, you try to make out the details of what's around you, but you can't. It's like you're blind. Sometimes when we are going about our day, taking in the scenes around us and hurrying from one thing to the next, we forget to stop and actually *see* the world. We become blind to the gifts that the Lord gives us daily. St. Celedonius, who was born blind, could still clearly see the world around him. He was able to recognize who Jesus was and share it with others.

Whenever you become too troubled with the stresses around you, think of St. Celedonius. He shows us that we can step outside of the darkness and live in the light of Christ. We can move beyond the fear or stress that might be distracting us and turn our eyes instead toward Jesus.

### Challenge of the Week

Think about the things that are making you anxious. Maybe it's an upcoming test, chores, or a recital. In these moments, consider praying the Rosary, or going on a Rosary walk, and contemplating the mystery for that day. Allow yourself to trust in the Lord that he will take care of your stresses and anxieties.

## Prayer of the Week

Lord, you revealed to St. Celedonius your true identity so that he could spread the good news of Christ. Help guide us to step out of the darkness to follow you. Help reveal to us your true identity so that we may be more like St. Celedonius, who saw you through his blindness. We ask this through our Lord, Jesus Christ. Amen.

## Bible Verse

"As he passed by, he saw a man blind from his birth. And his disciples asked him, 'Rabbi, who sinned, this man or his parents, that he was born blind?' Jesus answered, 'It was not that this man sinned, or his parents, but that the works of God might be made manifest in him. We must work the works of him who sent me, while it is day; night comes, when no one can work. As long as I am in the world, I am the light of the world'" (John 9:1–5).

## Song of the Week

**"Anima Christi"** (traditional hymn)

# Sight

*Read 1 Samuel 16:1b, 6–7, 10–13a;
Ephesians 5:8–14; John 9:1–41*

*"Once you were darkness, but now you are
light in the Lord; walk as children of light."*

## Reflect

I *love* this reading from the Gospel of John. The guy who was blind from birth is my hero. Even though he's been blind his whole life, he's able to see reality very clearly. What an absolute legend.

While I was starting a devotion to him, I found out that tradition tells us his name is St. Celedonius. He has so many of the admirable qualities of the saints. He trusts in Jesus' word; when Jesus smears clay on his eyes and tells him to go to the pool of Siloam to wash, he obeys—and his blindness is healed. This guy is so open and receptive, totally without guile and without fear of what others think of him. When the Pharisees question his healing, the man is courageous, truthful—and even hilarious in his response to the religious leaders: "Why, this is a marvel! You do not know where he comes from, and yet he opened my eyes" (John 9:30). He's also humble, allowing the Pharisees have their opinions without letting go of his own.

His most defining trait, however, is that he's able to *see*. The man who was blind from birth can see Jesus' identity so easily through this one miracle. St. Celedonius embodies the beatitude, "Blessed are the pure in heart, for they shall see God" (Matthew 5:8). He also embodies for us something of the effects of the Sacrament of Baptism; his going to wash in the pool of Siloam is a type of baptism, where his vision of God is fully restored. He shows the power of knowing your true identity, of a baptismal call that's lived out and owned!

Another interesting detail in this story is that St. John tells us that the name "Siloam" translates to "Sent" (see John 9:7). St. Celedonius ends up not only being sent to wash in the pool, but he is also, in a sense, sent out from there to evangelize. Jesus initially tells his disciples that this man was born blind "that the works of God might be made manifest in him" (John 9:3). Jesus gives him the gift of sight so that he might help others to see God's works more clearly. This man is repeatedly summoned and questioned by the Pharisees, even ridiculed by them for his belief in Jesus, and yet he just goes where he's directed and gives his answers firmly but charitably. He just "goes with the flow," so to speak, cooperating with God's grace and going where Jesus tells him to go.

The Pharisees, on the other hand, are blind to who Jesus is—and they remain blinded by their pride. Among other things, pride is the heart's attempt to create an identity for itself, to define itself apart from God. Because pride makes us set ourselves up in place of God, we can no longer recognize him, even when he is directly in front of us. We see Jesus having this effect on the hearts of the Pharisees, and as he says himself, "For judgment I came into this world, that those who do not see may see, and that those who see may become blind" (John 9:39). The religious leaders don't have the same humility that allows a man like

St. Celedonius to see Christ clearly. When Jesus asks him if he believes in the Son of Man, he responds with a question that springs from humility: "Who is he, sir, that I may believe in him?" (John 9:36).

Like St. Celedonius, we should give Jesus the room to reveal himself to us in the same way, not imposing our own ideas of who he is upon him, but letting him give us sight and clarity.

## Respond

In today's first reading, the Lord tells the prophet Samuel, "Do not look on his appearance or on the height of his stature, because I have rejected him; for the LORD sees not as man sees; man looks on the outward appearance, but the LORD looks on the heart" (1 Samuel 16:7). We continue with the theme from the end of last week of how God does not see things as we see them; his ways are above our ways. Ask him to help you see things as he sees them. Do you often get caught up in prioritizing superficial qualities in your judgments of others and yourself (beauty, social status, career, wealth, etc.)? Ask him to help you focus on looking into others' hearts and to stop comparing yourself to the limited knowledge of them that you can glean from the outside.

# Service

*Read Mark 9:30–50*

*"If any one would be first, he must be last of all and servant of all."*

### Reflect

In today's passage from Mark's Gospel, we read about the disciples' almost comical misunderstanding of Jesus' second prediction of his Passion. The prediction is worded very plainly, too—and yet his followers are too afraid to even ask for clarification. Instead of confronting this painful revelation, they change the subject and end up talking about which of them is the greatest.

It's easy for us to read this and laugh at their pettiness, believing that we would have obviously understood what Jesus was saying in the moment. Yet how many times do we end up in the same scenario? We're faced with countless examples of very real suffering every day, examples of Christ suffering in others. All you have to do is turn on the news to see a dozen such cases at once. There are plenty of people suffering in our own lives—even in our own homes—and yet we still get caught up in the same old traps: *Who is the greatest? How can I make myself the greatest?*

Often we'll see a story on social media about the evil going on in the world, and we'll think, *Oh man, that's terrible*—and then, a second later, we're back to scrolling through our newsfeed and comparing ourselves to others, trying to see who's the happiest, prettiest, richest, or who has the most perfect relationship. The Devil loves using such tactics, anything to distract us from focusing on what really matters, because if we actually look closely at the uncomfortable or scary realities of our broken world, we might actually be moved to start doing something about it and "getting our house in order."

Sometimes we have to be startled in order to wake up to the evil around us and to our own imperfections. Jesus uses some harsh imagery here, trying to impress upon his disciples how serious sin is. "If your hand causes you to sin, cut it off," he says—and "if your eye causes you to sin, pluck it out" (Mark 9:43, 47). That's ... not a fun thought. But Jesus isn't actually advocating for self-mutilation. He's trying to startle us out of our complacency and show us how ugly sin really is. He's pleading with us here, saying if we really knew—if we *really* were able to see how badly sin hurts us—we would realize that losing a limb is far better than suffering spiritual death from sin. The Devil knows that if we just keep sleeping, keep distracting ourselves by seeking greatness in superficial ways, we'll grow numb to the spiritual decay eating away at us and won't even notice it.

Jesus pulls the disciples' attention back to what we should really be focusing on: service. He calls us to serve the very, very least in society by using little children as an example. In Jesus' day, children really had no rights, power, or influence except through the love of their parents. They were truly dependent on others for everything in their lives. Jesus says that to serve someone as weak and dependent as a child is to serve him and his heavenly Father.

Can we accept his command to serve the very least—and can we do it in the most hidden way? Can we serve others with no bragging or virtue-signaling? Can we seek out, above all, that kind of service which won't look good on a résumé or in an Instagram post?

Notice how Christ does not condemn his disciples and say they shouldn't be worried about greatness at all. He only wants them to seek *true* greatness, not spend their time chasing after things that will ultimately fade. He wants to give us only the best without settling for anything less. If we want true greatness, who better to emulate than the King, the greatest in the Kingdom? Jesus is a king whose crowning glory was his ultimate sacrifice in service of all.

### Respond

What's a way that you tend to escape or numb yourself to painful realities? How do you think you can better confront them, courageously, without giving way to distraction?

_____

_____

_____

_____

_____

_____

_____

_____

_____

_____

# Commitment

*Read Mark 10:1–16*

*"For this reason a man shall leave his father and mother and be joined to his wife, and the two shall become one flesh."*

### Reflect

When I'm officiating at weddings, I like to tell the attendees that they are about to see one of the greatest shows on earth. It's like at the circus when the trapeze act would do the final performance with no safety net. The couple does the same thing—but it's with even greater risk, and it is so much more impressive.

Marriage on Jesus' terms, without divorce, *is* impressive. But what is most clear is that this requires God's power and help. As St. John Paul II wrote, "Marriage, the Sacrament of Matrimony, is a covenant of persons in love. And *love can be deepened and preserved only by Love*, that Love which is 'poured into our hearts through the Holy Spirit which has been given to us' (Rom 5:5)."[7] It's a challenging teaching, one which we can't carry out without grace.

Love is not content to sit still; it is always in motion. It's always striving towards some goal or another. That's why it's so important to have the same goal in mind before marriage—and that goal, hopefully, is to get each other to heaven.

The goal is not surviving marriage, but thriving, excelling in mutual love and entering into the joy of the gift of self. And Jesus tells us how to release this essential divine power: our childlike trust. Children trust by design. They are designed to trust their parents. In our lives, this looks like recognizing each day that we need God's help and then asking him for it. Getting his help is very simple—we need only ask.

No matter what your vocation is, you're called to that same sort of marital love. Christ is the spouse of our souls; in him, we are "one body and one Spirit" (Ephesians 4:4). We are tasked with that same sort of love that is always becoming a new creation. We're always renewing our commitment to him, and we should be striving to contribute to this love as much as Christ did. We see the extent of what he contributed every time we look at a crucifix. Are we willing to give as much for love as he did? Are we really all in?

Giving your life fully to Christ is a risky business. His is an all-or-nothing sort of love, and he wants the same from us: no safety net, no playing second fiddle to other loves in our lives. That demands a crazy level of trust and surrender, the level that only a child could attain. Parents tend to so many concerns while the child is completely oblivious to all of them. In the midst of a great many complicated problems, the child will just go on playing, will continue to be a lovable bundle of wants and needs, and will continue to trust that his parents will tend to all of them. We need to be the same with God—to be truly at rest in his arms, as the psalmist says:

> "O LORD, my heart is not lifted up,
> my eyes are not raised too high;
> I do not occupy myself with things
> too great and too marvelous for me.

But I have calmed and quieted my soul …
like a child that is quieted is my soul" (Psalm 131:1–2).

God does not promise an easy road. Then again, our growing relationship with God, like marriage, isn't an easy road. But like marriage, it's something we strive for anyway because the reward is worth the risk.

### Respond

Jesus says, "What therefore God has joined together, let not man put asunder" (Mark 10:9). This is true of marriage, but it's also true of other things. In this Lenten journey, we want to explore the truth that we are not just bodies and not just souls; we are a unity of both. Our nature is both material and spiritual. This is why we are doing both physical *and* spiritual exercises. As you exercise today, focus on it as a discipline that shows the holistic unity of your body and soul.

# Giving

### *Read Mark 10:17–31*

*"Jesus looking upon him loved him, and said to him, 'You lack one thing; go, sell what you have, and give to the poor, and you will have treasure in heaven; and come, follow me.'"*

### Reflect

This story is so heartbreaking! In today's passage, a man ran up to Jesus and asked him an important question: "Good Teacher, what must I do to inherit eternal life?" (Mark 10:17). This was a good man—he had pursued God his whole life, and Jesus saw that. He looked at him and *loved* him (see Mark 10:21). How could he walk away after receiving that look from Jesus?

That's the tragedy. This man had pursued God since his youth, never breaking the commandments or going astray from his faith. Even so, he could not let go of the one thing that kept him from fully giving himself to God: He could not surrender his material things. Ultimately, the man turns away from Jesus' love and goes away sorrowfully.

We must remember that Scripture is a mirror to help us better see ourselves. This same tragedy is repeated daily. Even as we recognize the tragedy in this story, we repeat it continually ourselves. Why do we do this? How is it that we're able to turn away from God even as he looks at us so lovingly? It's because we're looking at something else. In the case of this man, it's wealth. He recognizes that God is good, but he sees wealth as just a little bit more so.

He's not alone in this—in fact, the culture even backed him on that (what else is new?). Jewish beliefs of the time held that material prosperity was a sign of God's favor; that's why the disciples are so shocked when Jesus turns this teaching on its head. It's easy to see how one could go from seeing wealth as a sign of God's love to seeing it as a god in itself. When you can't see God in poverty and trials, you start to forget what his face looks like.

Whatever we make our god, if it isn't God himself, will hold us back because we need God's power to progress! God gives us good things to help us get to him and because he wants us to be happy. But he allows us to experience trials and tribulations because he loves us and wants to draw us even closer to himself. As close as this man was to the Kingdom of God, Jesus wanted to draw him even closer, but he couldn't give up that one last thing. He had an inverted ladder of loves, with God just below material goods.

St. Bonaventure wrote of St. Francis that he made a "ladder" out of all creation with which to climb up to the Creator:

> "In beautiful things
>   [St. Francis] saw Beauty itself
>   and through his *vestiges* imprinted on creation
>   *he followed his Beloved* everywhere,
>   making from all things a ladder

by which he could climb up
and embrace him *who is utterly desirable*."[8]

When we see the good of things like money, we mustn't stop there. We must ascend through gratitude to look at God's goodness, using earthly goods to climb higher towards Goodness himself.

This doesn't mean we have to throw everything away. However, we need to seek first the Kingdom, to detach our hearts from anything that we prize above God. With him, you get it all back: fathers, mothers, lands, and more. Fear not. You get the best interest rate in the universe: a hundredfold, a hundred times your investment—in other words, God himself.

## Respond

I find fasting most difficult when I focus on the food—or, actually, the lack of it. Then the hunger pangs kick in, and it's a grueling day. Instead, I try to focus on the positives: all the extra time I'll get if I'm not prepping food or eating (depending on the type of fast); how I'm spending more intimate time with God (which I try to do on fast days); the sharpness of my spirit that comes with a little self-denial; and having something to offer him who gives me so much. If I get trapped in obsessing about my hunger and weakness, then I turn back to Jesus and ask myself if I'd be willing to do it for love of him. Try focusing on that today, on your gratitude for having something a little bit more difficult than usual to offer to him.

# Haste

*Read Mark 10:32–45*

*"The Son of man also came not to be served but to serve, and to give his life as a ransom for many."*

## Reflect

Today we see Jesus walking ahead of his followers, hurrying toward Jerusalem. His followers are amazed and afraid at the same time. Why? Because he is rushing to his death. He makes his third prediction of this, describing how he will be mocked and spit upon and scourged—and still, he hastens on his way.

It's not that Jesus is in a rush. His pace communicates that he is busy with his Father's will and won't let anything get in the way of him doing it. He is zealous for it and anxious to fulfill his mission.

St. Luke uses the word for zeal in referring to Our Lady when she "went with haste into the hill country" to help Elizabeth (Luke 1:39); the shepherds also "went with haste" to see the child Jesus after receiving the message of the angels (Luke 2:16). In the original Greek, the word for "haste" used here—*spoudé*—also means "zeal," with a burning passion. Whether it's Mary, the shepherds, or Jesus making his way to Jerusalem, they go with zeal toward answering the Lord's call for them.

This zeal reveals the heart of Jesus, always burning with love for us, and this is the fire that spreads to those who live in his love. Think of the image of his Sacred Heart, always pictured as being on fire with love. In his apparitions to St. Margaret Mary Alacoque, he said, "Behold the Heart which has so loved men that it has spared nothing, even to exhausting and consuming Itself, in order to testify Its love."[9]

His heart burns with a fire that is catching; when he appears to the two disciples on the road to Emmaus and their eyes are opened to him, they say, "Did not our hearts burn within us while he talked to us on the road, while he opened to us the Scriptures?" (Luke 24:32). Even after having traveled all that way, they set out immediately and go all the way back to Jerusalem to share their news with the Eleven. If we're to partake in the Lord's mission, it's so important that we not allow ourselves to grow lukewarm in the faith. This is why St. Paul says, "Never flag in zeal, be aglow with the Spirit, serve the Lord" (Romans 12:11).

These themes of zeal and service are intertwined. Notice how, ever since Jesus declared his coming Passion, the theme of serving others has come up. After the second prediction, he says to serve the least; after today's third prediction, he tells us to serve all. This isn't just some random recommendation—this is Jesus' heart. In these chapters, he's really driving this point home. He's showing us how to imitate him, how to achieve the place closest to him in his Kingdom. We have this way open to us, to imitate Jesus in his death by dying to self and becoming the servant of all. Let us also go "with haste" to share his burning love with others.

## Respond

What are you most zealous about? What is the thing (or things) that truly ignites your heart with zeal and makes you set out with haste to accomplish your purpose? Does your heart burn within you in the same way on receiving God's Word? If they don't yet align with service, how might those other things that you're zealous about be tied into your service of God and others?

# Boldness

*Read Mark 10:46–52*

*"Jesus said to him, 'Go your way; your faith has made you well.' And immediately he received his sight and followed him on the way."*

## Reflect

In today's passage from Mark, once again we see that a blind man has clearer sight than many others. This man, Bartimaeus, knows that Jesus is the Son of David, and he cries out for Jesus to heal him. Even though others rebuke him and tell Bartimaeus to be silent, he is so confident in Jesus' identity that he refuses to let the words of others rattle him; he only cried out louder, "Son of David, have mercy on me!" (Mark 10:48).

We see such boldness from Bartimaeus. Such boldness can mean two things: either immense arrogance or great humility and freedom from the fear of man. The freedom from this fear is known as the fear of the Lord. To only care about what God thinks and wants is the ultimate freedom.

Those who were rebuking Bartimaeus change their tune instantly when Jesus summons him, and they tell him to take courage. Bartimaeus already has that courage. Even though others see him as an inconvenience or a disturbance along Jesus' way, Bartimaeus knows the heart of Christ better than they do. He knows that Jesus' heart is stirred with pity for his people, especially for the most afflicted and suffering. Jesus loves our boldness of faith; when we ask him out of the bold confidence of God's beloved children, it moves his heart.

The key, then, is to develop the fear of the Lord that is the "beginning of wisdom" (Proverbs 9:10) and produces this type of boldness. St. John Chrysostom teaches us,

> And how may this fear be produced? If we but consider that God is everywhere present, hears all things, sees all things, not only whatsoever is done and said, but also all that is in the heart, and in the depth of the soul, for He is *'quick to discern the thoughts and intents of the heart'* (Hebrews 4:12), if we so dispose ourselves, we shall not do or say or imagine anything that is evil. Tell me, if you had to stand constantly near the person of a ruler, would you not stand there with fear?[10]

St. John Chrysostom is saying that if you're always mindful of God's presence—when you eat, when you sleep, or when you are tempted to engage in some sort of sin—you will have the fear that comes from knowing that you're standing beside the King. Fear of the Lord is one of the gifts of the Holy Spirit; it brings us not to despair but to vigilance. St. John Chrysostom continues: "Do thou be bold; *'for it is God that works in you.'* If then He works, it is our part to bring a mind ever resolute, clenched and unrelaxed."[11]

Fear of the Lord makes us bold in service of the King; in service of the King, it makes all other considerations fall away. When Jesus calls Bartimaeus, St. Mark says that "throwing off his cloak he sprang up and came to Jesus" (Mark 10:50). Cloaks were an important article of clothing at the time; they gave protection from the elements and could double as a blanket at night. The fact that Bartimaeus throws it aside shows his complete reliance on Jesus and how greatly he makes haste to obey him. The King had called him, and now he has no other consideration. Jesus tells him, "Go your way," and Bartimaeus follows him. The King's way is his way.

## Respond

One of my biggest challenges is letting go of people and what they think of me. This is more rooted directly in vanity rather than pride, but both are from the same root of a self-love that leaves God out of the picture. Prayerfully reflect on whose approval you most desire in life or whose rejection you fear the most. It is natural to want approval and fear rejection, but they can get to a point where they stop us from acting in freedom and love when they are more powerful than our desire for God's approval. Surrender these to God in your own words and ask him for the grace to truly make him your number one in life.

# Fruit

*Read Mark 11:12–33*

*"As they passed by in the morning, they saw the fig tree withered away to its roots."*

## Reflect

Today's passage contains a very "Marcan" moment. Specifically, it shows us a side of Jesus that the other Gospels don't mention: Jesus curses a poor little fig tree for not bearing figs—even though figs were *out of season.* Not fair!

Before we judge this passage too quickly, we should remember that this example of the fig tree is not about Jesus being cross and "hangry." (Obviously, as we've seen from the multiplication of the loaves and fish, if he really wanted to, he could easily make the tree grow some figs instead of making it wither.) So, what is the bigger picture here?

As the Author of creation, Jesus is using nature not only to show his divinity but also to create a visible illustration of the spiritual corruption he's talking about. As we've seen from his parables and teachings, fruit is important to Jesus; it keeps coming up as a symbol for virtue, holiness, and faithfully living out God's Word. This cursing of the fig tree was a prophetic act on his part of what would happen to Jerusalem and Israel if they would not bear fruit. Just as Jesus walked up to this fig tree and expected fruit, he walks up to the Temple and expects fruit, holiness, and righteousness. He isn't happy with what he finds. In fact, as Jesus foretold, the Temple was destroyed in AD 70.

In the same way, Jesus is walking into the temple of our souls, hoping that we will bear fruit. We can't claim that it's not the season for fruit; it is *always* the season for fruit in the Kingdom of God. If he were to survey your soul, would he be happy with what he sees?

These scenes are bound together by a common theme: Jesus wants authentic faith. He can't stand hypocrisy. The Temple, which outwardly seemed a place to worship the one true God, was filled with people worshipping the false idol of money. The Pharisees, who were supposedly the exemplars of virtue, were more concerned with power and prestige.

When Peter and the other apostles marvel at how the fig tree withered, Jesus takes the opportunity to tell them that their faith must be authentic. If we recite the words of prayers and profess belief in God but don't really expect our prayers to have any real effect, our faith is not authentic. If we ask for God's mercy but don't forgive others, we show that we don't trust in God's judgment and think that we can judge better ourselves. We have the appearance of a tree that bears fruit, but we have nothing to show for our faith.

Jesus isn't just looking for a lack of sin, for the absence of the money changers in our temples. He wants the presence of virtue and especially of love. Do we seek each day to do acts of love for others—our family, friends, strangers, the poor, the sick, the imprisoned, immigrants, outcasts? Are we striving to perform the corporal and spiritual works of mercy? Let's make sure that when he comes to us, hungry for the fruit of our souls, he is greeted by the sight of a tree that bears good fruit.

Do you tend to view your life with the thought that it is not the season for fruit? In other words, are you content to do spring cleaning (chasing the money changers out of the Temple) but go easy on yourself in terms of actually bearing fruit (thinking you'll do it when you're happier, have more money, don't have so many things to worry about)? What is one way you can cultivate the fruit of holiness and service right now during Lent?

_____

_____

_____

_____

_____

_____

_____

_____

_____

_____

_____

_____

_____

_____

_____

_____

_____

_____

_____

_____

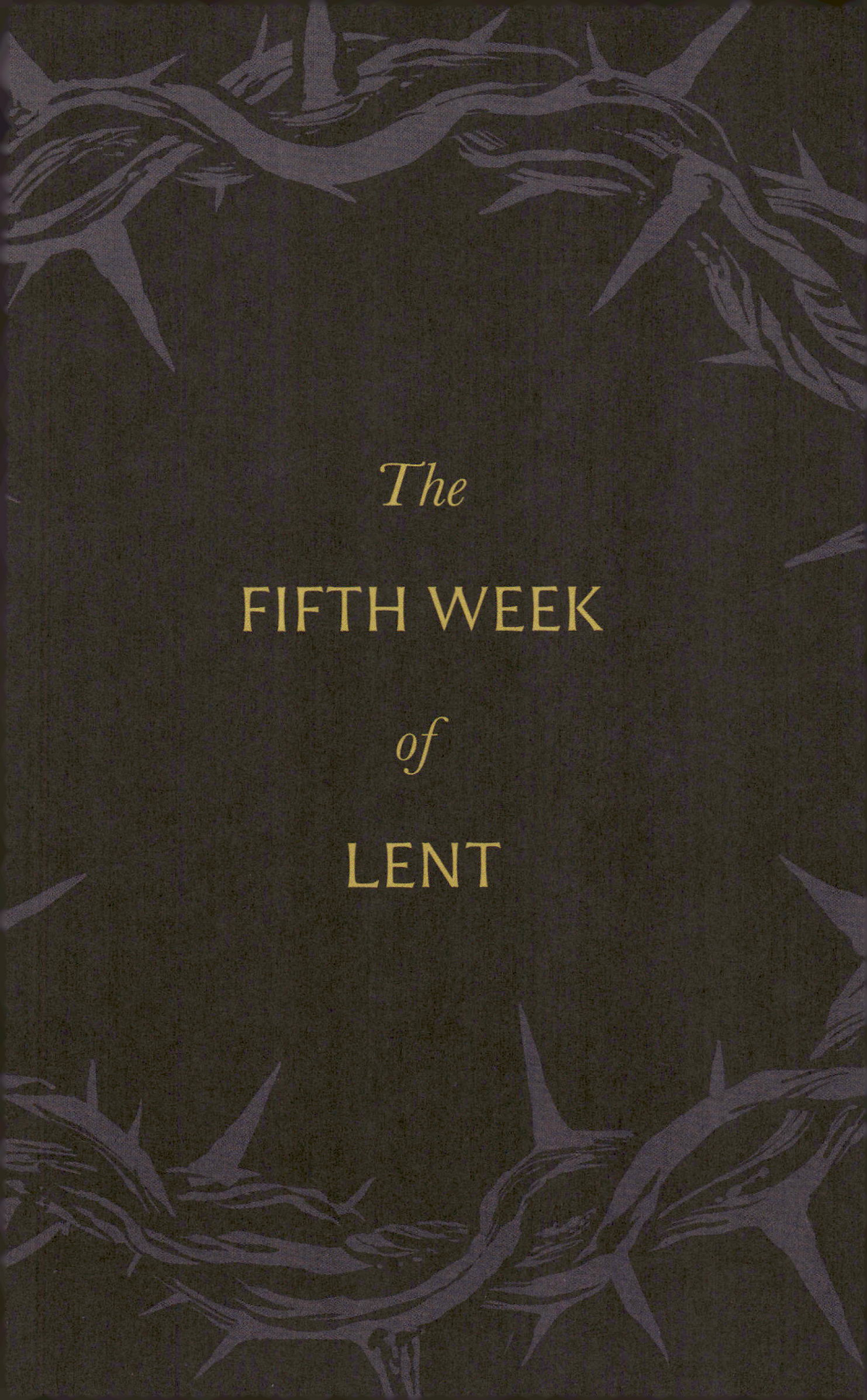

*The*

# FIFTH WEEK

*of*

# LENT

### The Fifth Week of Lent

This week, we hear about the death of Lazarus, and we see Martha and Mary's pain at the loss of their brother. When Jesus comes, Martha greets him by saying, "Lord, if you had been here, my brother would not have died" (John 11:21). Martha knew that Jesus could have saved Lazarus from death, and although it may sound like she's upset with Jesus, she says it with full trust in the Lord, knowing that he has the ability to save. The friendship that Jesus has with both Martha and Mary is a beautiful example of his humanity.

Friendship—and finding people to accompany you on your journey through Lent—is incredibly important. We are called to friendship and community because the Lord knows that it is sometimes harder for us to do something when we're alone. God will often put people in our lives to help us through a difficult time. Christ asks us to trust him, and like Martha, we need to believe that Christ has the ability to save. Through this belief, we can trust in the Lord's will and way with our lives.

## Challenge of the Week

Pray with a friend. Instead of going about your day alone, seek out a friend who might need comfort or a little encouragement. Offer to pray with or for them.

## Prayer of the Week

Lord, we are called into unity with you. You revealed to us the importance of friendship through Mary and Martha. Help us to be more like Martha and trust in Christ's ability to save. Allow us to continue this journey through Lent with a heart full of trust in your will and way, Lord. Help us define ourselves by you. We ask this through our Lord, Jesus Christ. Amen.

## Bible Verse

"Jesus said to her, 'Your brother will rise again.' Martha said to him, 'I know that he will rise again in the resurrection at the last day.' Jesus said to her, 'I am the resurrection and the life; he who believes in me, though he die, yet shall he live, and whoever lives and believes in me shall never die. Do you believe this?'" (John 11:23–26)

## Song of the Week

**"Change Our Hearts"** (Rory Cooney)

# Friendship

*Read Ezekiel 37:12–14; Romans 8:8–11; John 11:1–45*

*"Jesus wept. So the Jews said, 'See how he loved him!'"*

## Reflect

What amazing disciples Martha and Mary are! Jesus' affection for them is so great, and they know it. They are beloved, and they have a confidence that flows from this fact. Martha and Mary model this belovedness in their friendship with Jesus, but they also do something that's really difficult: They model friendship with God himself!

Friendship means that you enter into greater intimacy with someone. When it comes to having a friendship with God, though, our friendship with God leads not to familiarity but to deeper reverence. We see this interesting paradox highlighted in Jesus' friendship with Mary and Martha. I don't mean that in God we find conflicting truths; in him, we find that truths which seem incompatible are reconciled. He is all at once friend, brother, father, and king to us.

Because of this, we speak to God in a way that we speak to no one else. Martha says, "Lord, if you had been here, my brother would not have died" (John 11:21). This sounds like both a rebuke from a friend and also a statement of faith. In fact, all of Martha's statements are charged with a profound faith, and they draw further revelation out of Jesus that points to his divinity: Jesus tells her, "I am the resurrection and the life" (John 11:25). She speaks with a tone that is at once affectionate and also filled with humility and reverence; she is addressing Jesus as both her friend and Lord.

Mary takes the emotion to the next level. She says exactly the same line as Martha at first, but she finishes by weeping. Jesus does not rebuke her for emotionalism; he is profoundly moved, and he weeps, too. Mary's emotion and honesty reveal more of Jesus' humanity and affection. Martha shows us Christ's paradoxical relationship with us; Mary shows us Christ's paradoxical nature as God and man. These revelations point to a beautiful truth about friendship itself. In *The Four Loves*, C.S. Lewis writes, "In each of my friends there is something that only some other friend can fully bring out. By myself I am not large enough to call the whole man into activity; I want other lights than my own to show all his facets."[12] Different people reveal different facets of a person, and we are glad to be able to know our friends even more thoroughly through their friendships with others. This is especially true of friendship with the infinite God, about whom there is always more to learn.

We learn different things about God through Martha and Mary, and we see how listening to others talk about their relationship with God deepens our own knowledge of him. This is why there is such rejoicing in God's Kingdom whenever a new soul is admitted; the faith of others amplifies our own and gives both us and God such great joy!

## Respond

Are there any insights that other people have given you about the nature of God and his love? What insights have stuck with you? Think back to any times when someone else was talking about their own relationship with God and it deepened your own or made you marvel at God's work in our lives.

_____

_____

_____

_____

_____

_____

_____

_____

_____

_____

_____

_____

_____

_____

_____

_____

_____

_____

_____

_____

_____

_____

_____

_____

# Belonging

*Read Mark 12:1–17*

*"Render to Caesar the things that are Caesar's, and to God the things that are God's."*

## Reflect

It's an interesting thought experiment: If I were a coin, whose image would I bear? Who or what owns me? Who or what possesses me?

This passage is about two kinds of possession, really: We talk about demonic possession as well as belonging to God. They sound similar, but they are, of course, totally different. Both involve communion with a spirit—but the difference is that when we give ourselves to God, we find that he gives himself totally to us. We become unspeakably free in a way we never thought possible.

Sometimes we're confused about what true freedom is. We may think it means not belonging to anyone, not having to answer to anyone, and having no cares or responsibilities. True freedom, though, is not about having no connections or responsibilities, but is actually being able to choose the good. The *Catechism* says,

> The more one does what is good, the freer one becomes. There is no true freedom except in the service of what is good and just.

> The choice to disobey and do evil is an abuse of freedom and leads to 'the slavery of sin' (*cf.* Romans 6:17). Freedom makes man *responsible* for his acts to the extent that they are voluntary. Progress in virtue, knowledge of the good, and ascesis enhance the mastery of the will over its acts. (CCC 1733–1734)

By sinning, we willingly give ourselves over to evil. When we open the door and invite it in, we're not the ones in control, as we may think we are. The Devil works subtly; he starts by gaining a toehold, then a foothold, then a stranglehold. Though we are made in the image and likeness of God, the Devil works to tempt us so that our sin gradually effaces the image of God that is stamped upon our hearts. Satan would like nothing more than to replace God's image with his own.

Our fear of sacrifice, of belonging to others, and of responsibility are ways in which Satan tries to convince us that we bear no image at all. Sometimes we think that, in our natural state, we bear no image and belong to no one, but we always belong to something or someone; we don't exist in a vacuum. In this case, the idea of freedom itself becomes our false idol. If Satan can further convince us that we don't *want* to bear God's image because doing so would feel like bondage, his work is even easier! Satan would love for us to believe that God is making us follow his rules and sacrifice our desires just for the heck of it—even though in reality, God does these things only so that he can give us something better.

When we are free from sin, when we are no longer controlled by our passions and enslaved by our desires, we are able to delight in what is true, good, and beautiful. By losing ourselves in Christ, we become more fully ourselves. He wants us to be that way, because when we are who he created us to be, we not only are happier ourselves but also bring joy to the heart of the

Divine Artist who made us! He created us for happiness with himself and with others. That's what heaven is, and we attain it by loving God and others here on earth.

Remember whose image you bear. Remember to whom you belong. You belong to God, not to the powers of darkness. When others around you forget that they bear that image, too, remind them of this beautiful truth, if not in words, then in loving them well.

### Respond

Can you think of someone in your life who needs reminding of their worth and dignity in Christ, of the fact that they are made in God's image and likeness? How can you find new ways to remind them of this fact and impress this truth upon them?

_____

_____

_____

_____

_____

_____

_____

_____

_____

_____

_____

_____

_____

_____

_____

# Receptivity

*Read Mark 12:18–27*

*"He is not God of the dead, but of the living; you are quite wrong."*

## Reflect

Today's passage is the only verbal conflict between Jesus and the Sadducees recorded in St. Mark's Gospel. The Sadducees were a Jewish sect that, like the Pharisees, were critical of Jesus and his teachings. Unlike the Pharisees, however, the Sadducees accepted only the written Law of Moses (the Torah) and rejected all later revelation. They did not uphold oral tradition and denied doctrines such as the eternity of the soul, the resurrection of the body, and the existence of angels.

When the Sadducees confront Jesus with a seemingly impossible scenario about heaven and marriage, Jesus manages to pretty much confound all their denials in the shortest argument possible, using both reason and Scripture. In response, Jesus quotes God's words to Moses in the book of Exodus: "I am the God of Abraham, and the God of Isaac, and the God of Jacob" (Mark 12:26; see Exodus 3:6). Jesus points out how God uses the present tense verb—"I am," not "I was"—which shows that the patriarchs are alive and pointing to the immortality of the soul. Based on the Jewish holistic view of the human person as body and soul, they will be reunited with their bodies in the resurrection of the body. Jesus' simile comparing our heavenly life to being "like the angels" subtly shows how complete the Sadducees' misunderstanding is. They can't understand what life in heaven will be like because all their ideas are tethered to earthly realities. Though God had spoken to his people through his prophets many times, the Sadducees rejected much of the Scripture that would have given them a fuller understanding of the human person and heaven. God had spoken and offered understanding, but they had rejected it.

God has great answers to all of our questions, but we need to ask them humbly. Humility is what softens our hearts and makes us receptive; it allows God's word to take root within us. Without it, no matter how much we read Scripture or study the works of the saints, the words will glance off our hardened hearts and won't find a home there. So much of our misunderstanding stems from our assumption that, when we're confused, it's because God hasn't revealed enough to us. It would help if we started with the opposite assumption: namely, that God has already answered our questions, and we either didn't recognize his voice, didn't look for a response in the right place, or outright rejected his word.

When we do know what God's word is and still struggle with it, we need to pray for the Holy Spirit's aid in accepting and understanding his word. With humility, we can recognize that there is wisdom in all that he does, and it is our own judgment that is lacking. We also need to be patient in waiting for illumination to come. If we don't understand a teaching of the Church right away, even after praying, we just need to be patient and make sure our hearts are softened and ready to accept his word. Are we sure that we want the Holy Spirit's help in understanding? Or do we grumblingly resign ourselves to follow particular teachings while still thinking our ways are better?

God wants us to ask questions of him not from a desire to test him but from a genuine desire to get to know him better. He always answers those who earnestly seek him: "O that today you would listen to his voice! Harden not your hearts" (Psalm 95:8).

## Respond

What would your life look like if exercising became a habit and was a spiritual practice? Do you feel this becoming a habit? Is it getting easier? If it's not settling in as a habit yet, you could think about becoming even more regular with the time of day (such as when you wake up or right before breakfast or dinner), or you could combine it with another habit you've already established. Introducing more order into our schedules not only makes it easier to remember to do things but also gives us more time than we think we have by ensuring it's not wasted on frivolous things.

# Understanding

*Read Mark 12:28–37*

*"When Jesus saw that he answered wisely, he said to him, 'You are not far from the kingdom of God.'"*

## Reflect

In today's passage from Mark 12, Jesus provides a perfect summary of the entire Law in just two statements. The first part of this Great Commandment is that you shall love God with all of your heart, all your soul, all your mind, and all your strength. This comes from the Old Testament: "Hear, O Israel: The LORD our God is one LORD; and you shall love the LORD your God with all your heart, and with all your soul, and with all your might" (Deuteronomy 6:4–5). This is so good, so powerful. I translate the commandment to mean that my love of God must involve my emotions, my will, my thoughts, my deeds, and my words.

The opposite of this is hypocrisy. Hypocrisy is where we say one thing and mean the other, loving (supposedly) with words or actions but unloving in heart and thought. God demands a love that is integrated and pure. To go against this means we put something else in the place which ought to be his; if we are not giving him our whole heart, it is because something else has a hold of it. Whether it's our own plans or desires for our life, our love of material goods, or even of other people, something else has become a false idol to us.

This is why the Great Commandment builds upon the first of the Ten Commandments: "You shall not have other gods besides me" (Exodus 20:3 NAB). To truly follow the First Commandment, we can't just refrain from worshipping strange gods or false idols. We have to actively love and worship the one, true God.

Beyond this, Jesus gives us the second part of this Great Commandment: "Love your neighbor as yourself" (Mark 12:31). How do we best do this? The scribe we encounter in today's passage gives us a great example. First, let's contrast this guy with the Sadducees: Whereas the Sadducees approached Jesus with their own prejudices and sought only to tear him down, this scribe approaches Jesus without bias and is receptive to his words. This is how Israel should have received the Messiah, and indeed, many in Israel did receive him this way, with great humility and a lack of prejudice.

Prejudice means to have judged a thing or person without knowing or encountering them. Because we know ourselves so well, we often make excuses for ourselves that we don't extend to others. Knowing our own hearts, we are quick to excuse behaviors in ourselves, thinking that if only others could see into our hearts, they would understand and would excuse us, too. We don't as often apply this logic to others, though; we mistakenly believe our limited view of them is enough to form "accurate" judgments. But the scribe in today's passage has a genuine encounter with Jesus, asking him a sincere question and withholding judgment until he answers. Jesus commends him for his understanding not just of the Law but of Christ himself.

We so desperately long to be understood; God wants understanding from us, too, and he wants us to also meet others with compassion and understanding. How do we set about doing this? Think of a truth about God or the Kingdom. Engage your emotions: to recognize that a truth is good is to love that truth. Feel that love. Then feel your desire for that truth—feel joy at it and engage other emotions. Then engage your will by choosing to love him in that moment, regardless of your feelings. Choose to align your will with his today, to surrender your to-do list and schedule, giving him permission to inspire and interrupt it as he wishes. Then commit to action—resolve to speak only out of love for him and others this day and to do what pleases him. Finally, do acts of charity out of love. The goal is to unite all of these faculties in prolonged acts of loving God and others. Obedience to the other commandments will flow naturally from this love.

## Respond

We fulfill so many of our desires automatically throughout the day without even realizing that they are luxuries rather than needs. It's not until we look for something to sacrifice that we realize how attached we are to creamer in our coffee, automatically turning on a show during meals, and listening to music in the car. The more we practice *not* fulfilling our desires by fasting, the easier it can become to resist them. In fact, resisting desire in low-stakes areas can actually assist us in resisting temptation overall. The more we practice placing God first in the everyday things, the easier it becomes to place him first in the big things. Practice giving up one such thing today with the intention of reordering your love for this thing in your life so that your love of God comes first.

# Generosity

*Read Mark 12:38–44*

*"Truly, I say to you, this poor widow has put in more than all those who are contributing to the treasury."*

## Reflect

The widow's mite is one of my favorite stories in the whole Gospel. What a woman. While others around her are giving financial gifts taken from their standing wealth, she instead gives *everything*, holding back nothing. What a beautiful example of faith and generosity!

The widow didn't know it, but she was seen by the living God, and he was stirred. He was so stirred that he immediately taught his disciples through her actions, which made it into three Gospel accounts.

Personally, I might be too ashamed to give such a small amount. I'd probably rather wait until I had something substantial to give. But this is perfectionism, when we believe that we have to get it all perfect before we come to God. We fall into the trap of thinking that we have to be just a little more spiritually "tidied up" before we can approach him and let him see us, and we let that stand in the way of growing in our relationship with him *now*. It doesn't work, anyway; we can't grow without him, so there's not much point in thinking we can come to him only once we have a bigger gift of virtue to show for ourselves.

There's also a different type of fear we can fall into. If I were in the widow's place, I would possibly be focused on my poverty in fear. I might worry about meeting my basic needs first; once I was secure enough, *then* I could get serious about God. "First things first," as they say. In this case, God is seen as a luxury, not an essential. This worry over having "enough" is what ultimately leads us to self-reliance. I know that in my own case, I can fall into self-reliance out of fear, totally taking my eyes off God and not trusting in his providence at all. However, our giving to God and others should always involve a deep trust that Our Father will provide for us even more generously. If we only give from our surplus once all our own needs and wants are covered, we're not practicing true generosity. If we view our wealth ultimately as a gift from God that we give back to him, with interest (namely, the good deeds that we do with the gifts he lends to us), he will all the more abundantly provide for us.

My offering, while it might seem pathetic compared to the offerings of others, is deeply pleasing to God—not because of the sum itself but because of the love with which it is given. That's all God asks of us. In fact, it is because the poor widow gave her all that she received Jesus' attention and admiration here. Of all the large and impressive sums that others gave that day, the only quantity St. Mark found worth recording was that of two small coins. At the end of the day, those two coins were worth more than all the other offerings.

All we give in love is multiplied by God. Jesus himself tells us how much God loves to give us good things: A "good measure, pressed down, shaken together, running over, will be put into your lap" (Luke 6:38). Give all you have, and you will always find that God cannot be outdone in generosity. He has an endless store to draw from and infinite love through which he gives.

## Respond

What does it mean to be drawn closer to God? For St. Ignatius of Loyola, it usually meant some form of consolation. Being drawn closer can also mean that we observe a silent fruit in our lives, a greater alignment with God's thinking and will. As we approach the final length of our journey through Lent, it may be helpful to start to look for the most dominant and clear ways that we have felt drawn closer to God. This can reveal to us the regular ways God speaks to us, which is very helpful. Meditate on the ways you've felt God drawing you closer so far this Lent.

# Perseverance

*Read Mark 13:1–23*

*"You will be hated by all for my name's sake. But he who endures to the end will be saved."*

## Reflect

The Olivet Discourse, which takes place here in today's passage from Mark, is about two things: one, the destruction of the Temple and Jerusalem in AD 70; and two, the end of the world in the future. The Temple's destruction proved the truth of Jesus' word, and now we wait with vigilance for the fulfillment of the other part of his prophecy.

In John's Gospel, Jesus tells the Jews, "Destroy this temple, and in three days I will raise it up" (John 2:19), referring to the destruction of the temple of his body. In judgment upon Jerusalem, the Temple, which had been the center of Jewish life, was destroyed by Roman legions in AD 70. The destruction of this Temple was a sign of the eventual destruction of the world—the Last Judgment yet to come, which we will all face at the end of time. Only the Father knows when this judgment will take place. In the meantime, though, we don't need to panic. We just need to take Jesus' advice: pray, be watchful, and persevere.

Jesus offers his disciples a glimpse of what they can expect for following him, and he paints a vivid picture. He tells them they will be handed over, beaten, put to death, and hated by all because of his name. This is... not the greatest advertisement for discipleship. In fact, nearly all of the apostles died a martyr's death (except for John), and all of them were tortured. In the face of that kind of evil, how can we keep from being afraid?

Simple: We must keep Christ's light before our eyes and keep God between us and darkness. In her famous "bookmark" prayer, St. Teresa of Ávila writes, "Let nothing disturb you, / Let nothing frighten you, / All things are passing away: / God never changes."[13] In the midst of things passing away, even of our own lives passing away, we cling to what is eternal. St. Teresa also says, "God withholds Himself from no one who perseveres."[14] If we persevere, even if we lose all else, we are guaranteed to have him, the one thing that will never change or pass away.

In tomorrow's reading, Jesus speaks of "this generation" (Mark 13:30); this refers to a period of 40 years, which is also taken to be a lifespan for many people back then. Lent, which is 40 days (plus seven for the Sundays of Lent), is therefore a mini-representation of our tiny lifespan. Just as our lives, and the world itself, will eventually come to an end, so too this Lent will end. Lent can serve as a small preparation for the bigger, lifelong work we have of preparing for our end. We are supposed to learn from this Lenten experience, to take our daily pilgrimage with Jesus just as seriously each day of Ordinary Time. Today, let's renew our commitment to living our lives intentionally for Jesus and to growing daily in our love for him. Let's persevere to the end so that we can say we have run well the race.

## Respond

In the interest of always being prepared, we generally have first aid kits or emergency supply kits in case of injury or physical threats. How can you always be spiritually prepared for the end of your life or of the world? What kinds of spiritual "tools" would you fall back on? Would you behave differently if you thought the world would end in the near future (e.g., go to confession more, pray the Rosary more regularly, go to daily Mass)?

# Watch

*Read Mark 13:24–37*

*"From the fig tree learn its lesson: as soon as its branch becomes tender and puts forth its leaves, you know that summer is near. So also, when you see these things taking place, you know that he is near, at the very gates."*

## Reflect

Today's passage is a continuation of Jesus' prophecy about the end times. Why did Jesus say that this generation would not pass away before all this had taken place (see Mark 13:30)? The world certainly hasn't ended yet. Can Jesus have been mistaken?

As we discussed yesterday, a generation was taken to mean 40 years. Some scholars argue that these words were spoken as early as AD 30, which is exactly 40 years—a generation—before the Temple's destruction in AD 70. From a Jewish point of view, the Temple was a sort of mini-cosmos, taken to represent the entirety of creation. To highlight this, the Temple walls were decorated with paintings of the Garden of Eden, and it had stars, the moon, and the sun painted on the ceiling. When Jesus says that the stars will fall from the sky (see Mark 13:25), this was symbolically achieved when the Temple collapsed at the hand of the Roman general Titus. For the Jewish people, the

Temple's destruction amounted to the end of the world—and the Temple's destruction also prefigures the true end of the world.

We've lived through the seasons enough times that, by now, we can detect the first subtle signs of spring—or we can look to the first hints of autumn that tell us when we need to bring out our cold-weather clothes. Jesus has told us that just as we know what to look for with nature's changing seasons, there are also signs that will point to the ultimate change of seasons with the end times. We also already saw how the early Christians lived through this first destruction of the "mini-cosmos"; they acted on Jesus' words and fled. We, too, know the type of destruction that is coming. Our job then is to watch, to "be sober, be watchful" (1 Peter 5:8), so that when the season changes, it may find us dressed appropriately.

Jesus gives us a simple, one-word command to conclude his prophecy: "Watch" (Mark 13:37). He doesn't give us a long list of instructions for doomsday preparations because so many things flow from just being watchful. If you are watchful, if you always keep before you an awareness of your end and of God's sovereignty, your conduct will reflect this awareness. There are two senses in which Jesus tells us to watch. First, we are called to watch with longing for his Second Coming. We are told by the Church to eagerly desire and hope for this—even to pray for it daily. The second sense is to watch over ourselves lest we admit any false messiahs or sins into the temple of our souls. We remain vigilant and watch for temptation such that even if we are laid siege to, like Jerusalem, by God's grace we can remain faithful till the end.

We don't want to let the flame of our faith go out, to become lukewarm and complacent so that the Lord comes and finds us sleeping. Instead, we keep our lamps trimmed and the flame of our faith burning brightly so that when the Bridegroom comes, we won't miss him.

## Respond

Sit down and plan your Holy Week now. Do you feel prompted to do something different this Holy Week? Check your parish's Holy Week schedule: What prayer services or opportunities are available this week at your parish or in your diocese (the Chrism Mass, confession, the Stations of the Cross, Triduum services, Tenebrae, the Easter Vigil, etc.)? What can you make time for this week to help you transition from Lent into Easter?

_____

_____

_____

_____

_____

_____

_____

_____

_____

_____

_____

_____

_____

_____

_____

_____

_____

_____

*Holy*

WEEK

# FOR THE
# FAMILY

## Holy Week

Holy Week is finally here! As we begin to prepare ourselves for Christ's Passion, let us remind ourselves first of how joyful it was when Jesus entered Jerusalem. Everyone was excited, laying palms on the ground for him. Still, even though he was being celebrated then, Jesus knew that in a few days those cries for his glory would turn into shouts for his death.

Have you ever sacrificed something for the sake of someone else? Maybe it was taking the blame for something wrong, even when you weren't the only one to blame—or maybe it was sticking up for someone when they were being bullied. Even though we might be tempted to be prideful in the moment—thinking to ourselves that we *deserve* something because we made that sacrifice—we have to stop ourselves and remain humble like Christ.

---

### Challenge of the Week

As we draw closer to Christ's Passion, look back on the list/drawing you created at the start of Lent. Reflect on what you did well this season and where you struggled. For these final days of Lent, take time to more actively do the tasks that you've neglected during Lent (such as doing a chore you don't enjoy or helping someone out).

## Prayer of the Week

Lord, as we enter into Holy Week, prepare our hearts to meet you in your suffering. Allow us to partake in your Passion and reveal to us your merciful heart. Help guide us in these final days of Lent so that we may not be tempted into neglecting our relationship with you. We ask this through our Lord, Jesus Christ. Amen.

## Bible Verse

"They brought the colt to Jesus, and threw their garments on it; and he sat upon it. And many spread their garments on the road, and others spread leafy branches which they had cut from the fields. And those who went before and those who followed cried out, 'Hosanna! Blessed is he who comes in the name of the Lord! Blessed is the kingdom of our father David that is coming! Hosanna in the highest!'" (Mark 11:7–10)

## Song of the Week

**"Jesus, Remember Me"**
(Jacques Berthier, Taizé chant)

# Humility

*Read Mark 11:1–11*

*"Those who went before and those who followed cried out, 'Hosanna! Blessed is he who comes in the name of the Lord!'"*

## Reflect

Holy Week is finally here! Today, on Palm Sunday, Jesus enters Jerusalem, and the crowds go wild! They think they're hailing the arrival of a great conqueror in a worldly sense; here is the Messiah, the one who is destined to overthrow Rome and establish an earthly kingdom. *Hosanna!*

But the crowds have a different understanding of this moment than Jesus does. Instead of a powerful warhorse fit for a conquering king, Jesus rides in on a baby donkey. We don't have donkeys where I live, but plenty of my neighbors have ponies—even some very small ones. Someone sitting on the back of such a small pony is bound to look a little silly. In the same way, it's impossible for a grown man like Jesus to sit on a baby donkey and not look humble. Jesus is in no way exalting himself here; instead, he is doing the opposite.

If life sometimes brings us glory and praise, we should take it with a grain of salt. Jesus knew that in a few days, the same crowds would be crying for his blood. However, he doesn't sneak into

Jerusalem, because much of the praise was rightly placed. Still, he doesn't receive the cheers with arrogance—only humility.

I once heard a story about an encounter between St. Teresa of Calcutta and the late Fr. Benedict Groeschel, CFR. When they entered a gathering together, greeted with loud cheering and applause, Mother Teresa turned to Fr. Groeschel and said, "Don't inhale." In other words, we shouldn't inhale the praise and adulation of others. Even when we win the esteem of virtuous people whom we hold in high regard, if we prize their good opinion too much, it can be dangerous to the heart trying to guard itself against pride.

But this doesn't mean that we should only do good deeds when no one is watching for fear of praise and accolades. Humility doesn't demand that we hide ourselves away; in fact, true Christian witness demands that we put our light on a lampstand for all to see (see Matthew 5:15). Rather, humility is recognizing your place and esteem in relation to God and others. The Christian life lived authentically is conspicuous; it's dynamic, fueled by a heart on fire with the faith—and if you're on fire, people are bound to notice. However, with humility we recognize that we can do nothing apart from God.

Jesus, again, is the one who gives us the example to follow. As St. Paul teaches us,

> Have this mind among yourselves, which was in Christ Jesus, who, though he was in the form of God, did not count equality with God a thing to be grasped, but emptied himself, taking the form of a servant, being born in the likeness of men. And being found in human form he humbled himself and became obedient unto death, even death on a cross. (Philippians 2:5–8)

Jesus was a natural leader; he had such a magnetic character that crowds followed him wherever he went. When he tells us to follow him, it's not because he lacks humility and wants fame and glory. It's because he is the light of the world, and he earnestly wants our happiness.

With humility, we recognize our strengths as well as our weaknesses, but we realize that those gifts and talents ultimately come from God. As Christians, we want others to see the light of Christ in us, but only so that they themselves may come to love Christ, not so that we can impress them with our piety. Like Jesus, we should employ our gifts in the service of others, letting our light shine brightly before all so that we can lead them to the source of that light.

### Respond

Pride makes us quick to see the faults in others, while humility makes us quick to notice their virtues. Do you tend to focus more on the faults or virtues of others? Is there someone in particular whom you tend to look at critically or maybe gossip or complain about? Draw out their virtues in your mind, and think of how you can exalt them, both in your own eyes and in the eyes of others.

# Meekness

*Read Mark 14:1–9*

*"Truly, I say to you, wherever the gospel is preached in the whole world, what she has done will be told in memory of her."*

### Reflect

In today's passage, we jump from Jesus' triumphal entry into Jerusalem in Mark 11 to the anointing at Bethany in Mark 14. Jesus has come to the house of Simon the leper; while he is there, a woman comes with a precious alabaster jar filled with the highest quality ointment—and she breaks the jar and dumps the contents over Jesus' head.

The anointing at Bethany wasn't just costly because of the pure nard (also called spikenard), which was so expensive that it cost almost a year's wages (wow!). It also came at the cost of this woman's reputation, as many of those present were indignant with her actions and criticized her. Consider how it must have felt for the woman to face opposition from all sides—from those in authority, her peers, and maybe even supposed friends. While this woman had only the purest of intentions (performing an act of love and devotion to her Lord), she finds her actions completely misinterpreted. Her love and generosity are construed as wastefulness and selfishness; if she had been truly generous, they say, she would have given that money to the poor (see Mark 14:4–5).

It seems to me that the criticism of her is like calling her vain or a fanatic. The people who believed her to be a fanatic would probably define the term as "anyone who loves God more than me." But if we look at the actions of the woman in today's reading, we can tell that she's not looking for praise or attention. She's not anointing Jesus in the hopes that one day, as Jesus says, what she has done will be told in memory of her throughout the whole world (see Mark 14:9). She's not trying to memorialize herself; she's trying to honor the Christ. She's just giving to Jesus what is owed to him.

The fact that other people are there has no bearing on the event; we are getting a glimpse into an intimate moment in this woman's personal relationship with Christ. She is inspired to do this act of homage and bear witness to her faith—and as we can see, she is not deterred by the fact that many who are present grew annoyed with her. The reactions of others are irrelevant to her. Jesus, too, seeing the purity of this woman's intentions, does not stop her from making this gesture, because she is giving him what is rightly owed: namely, her heart. It doesn't matter whether bystanders approve of the way in which it is given. This gift of her heart is what matters.

Today, let's envision the scene in prayer. In your mind, picture Jesus sitting at a table. It's the final week before his death, and it's Passover time. Where do you fit? Are you the host, the woman, a disciple, or someone else? Next, picture the woman coming in with the jar. What does she look like? Is she sad with repentance, or is she joyful? Watch her break the jar and pour the ointment, a whole year's wages, on Jesus' head. It's very messy. Jesus is covered with it—hair, face, clothes. The table and ground around him are covered. How do people react? How do *you* react? Next, someone speaks out in criticism. Listen and observe your heart's reaction. Listen and watch as Jesus defends her. Finally, Jesus turns to you. What do you have to say in response to this moment?

## Respond

Meekness subjects our passions—anger, disappointment, frustration—to reason and helps us to respond with gentleness and love. Jesus does not reply to the woman's critics with hatred; he acknowledges the good aspect of their criticism (care for the poor) and tries to instruct them by helping them see the goodness of the woman's actions, too. What is your typical response to insults or things that anger you? Is your immediate response one of indignation and rage? How can you temper your reply, whether on your own behalf or that of others, so that your response is dictated not just by a desire to vindicate yourself but also by a love of the other person and a desire to be united with them in Christ?

_____

_____

_____

_____

_____

_____

_____

_____

_____

_____

_____

# Brother

*Read Mark 14:10–11*

*"Judas Iscariot, who was one of the Twelve, went to the chief priests in order to betray him to them."*

*Reflect*

This is the shortest passage from Mark for our entire Lenten journey—yet so much is being said in these three sentences! Yesterday, we read about the woman who poured out her gift of nard worth three hundred denarii. Jesus has poured so much more into Judas: his time, his teaching, his love. He gave three years of his life on earth to Judas and, most importantly, counted him among his closest friends.

Given what we know of Judas' reaction to the woman anointing Jesus from other Gospels (see Matthew 26:6–13; Luke 7:36–50; John 12:1–8), Judas' act of betrayal seems to have been inspired in direct response to this woman's costly gift and Jesus' defense. This is so much like the story in Genesis 4 of Cain and Abel, the sons of Adam and Eve. Abel's worship was pleasing to God, whereas Cain's was not—so Cain, sick with envy, killed his brother. Cain had the heart of a man who felt fear from scarcity and rejection, who didn't understand that he was already a son. Cain fell prey to the belief that because his brother's offering was well received, he somehow couldn't be loved as much, as if there wasn't enough love to go around. In this thought process, worship turns into a competition. Maybe Judas, like Cain, was envious of how this woman's offering was received by Jesus. Maybe he felt humbled by Jesus' words in defense of this woman and felt that his own efforts to follow Jesus were inadequate by comparison.

Matthew 26:15 gives us a few more details about Judas' betrayal. Matthew tells us that Judas betrayed Jesus for thirty pieces of silver. Think of what this tells us about how much Judas valued his friendship with Christ. He was willing to throw it all away for so little. Contrast this with how much the woman at Bethany values her friendship with Christ, spending 300 denarii just for one act of worship. She paid that much for just a couple of moments; Judas accepted a tenth of that price to throw away a friendship of three years!

There is a great lesson here about the importance of not comparing ourselves to others, especially when it comes to our relationship with God. God loves each of us so uniquely and speaks to each of us in different ways. It's dangerous to look at the spiritual consolations that others receive and think that because we're not receiving the same, God doesn't love us. In envying them, we shut ourselves off from listening to what God is trying to tell us. We basically tell God that he's not loving us as he should.

Envy requires that I first believe that I am *not* loved or lovable in some way. With one little comparison, one little show of love or excellence by anyone, I'm enraged. Believing this initial lie, namely that we are not loved or lovable, causes such immense pain and pulls us away from God. It eats away at our hearts until we are willing even to betray Love himself because we think he is not willing to receive us. How many of those around us have fallen prey to this lie? How often do we ourselves give in to it?

## Respond

The antidote to envy is fraternal charity, which enables us to rejoice in the joys and successes of others. Our individual journeys to God won't look exactly the same, and we can rejoice in the beautiful ways in which God writes others' stories. Think of someone you frequently compare yourself to or maybe envy. What traits do you admire about them that you can work on developing in yourself? How do you see God doing beautiful things in that person's life, and how can you offer him praise for his work as the Divine Author?

# Rejection

*Read Mark 14:12–21*

*"Truly, I say to you, one of you will betray me."*

## Reflect

It's something we know so well that we have likely forgotten how startling this fact is: Jesus *chose* Judas to be one of his closest followers. Jesus ordains Judas as an apostle. He breaks bread and shares the Passover meal with Judas at the Last Supper. Just like all his other apostles, Jesus keeps loving Judas "to the end" (John 13:1); sadly, Judas could not let this love in.

We can never know for certain why Jesus included Judas as one of the Twelve, even though one day Judas would betray him. Perhaps it was because of his own teaching; he wanted to demonstrate how it's no credit to us if we only love those who love us in return. He wanted to show us a different way: "But I say to you, Love your enemies and pray for those who persecute you" (Matthew 5:44). Jesus wanted to show us what it means to give everything to another, even someone who would betray him in the end. It's not that Jesus wanted Judas' rejection or caused it to happen somehow. No, he accepted it as an act of Judas' free will—and he brought good from it so that he could give us an example of the highest form of love until the end.

This is love. This is what it means to will the other's good, no matter how they choose to respond to that love. Jesus cannot or will not make us love him, but he can choose to continue to love us, as he did with Judas.

This kind of love is far from easy. For Jesus, it came at tremendous cost. In her diary, the mystic St. Faustina wrote Jesus' words to her one day: "My daughter, I want to rest in your heart, for many souls have cast Me out of their hearts today; I have been made mortally sad."[15] Knowing this, will you let his love find a home in your heart? Will you seek to console him? By letting him love you, you console his heart and make up for others who have perhaps, for a time, gone the way of Judas—those who have rejected Jesus in their heart.

During Our Lady's apparitions at Fatima, an angel gave the children a prayer that we should all pray every day to make an act of reparation for the unbelief in the world: "My God, I believe, I adore, I hope, and I love You! I beg pardon for those who do not believe, do not adore, do not hope, and do not love You."[16] The angel said that to live our lives according to this prayer is to have the theological virtues of faith, hope, and charity.

Let us pray for those who have rejected Jesus, and let us receive Jesus and his love as fully into our hearts as possible this Holy Week.

### Respond

Think of a time in your life when you experienced betrayal. How did you react? How do you think Christ would have responded in the same situation? Can you say today that you still earnestly desire that person's good and that you want to be united with them in heaven?

# Suffering

*Read Mark 14:22–72*

*"Abba, Father, all things are possible to you; remove this chalice from me; yet not what I will, but what you will."*

*Reflect*

When I first started to believe in Jesus at age seventeen, while I was learning more about the lives of the saints, I started to get the impression that I needed to seek out suffering. My mother quite wisely redirected my enthusiasm by saying that I shouldn't worry; she told me that I didn't have to go looking for suffering, because suffering would eventually find me. She was right: One year later, my brother died of a brain infection.

Life always involves suffering. Suffering is ultimately a result of living in the world after the Fall. Because of our fallen nature and disordered desires, embracing God's will often means embracing or experiencing suffering in some form.

The Last Supper and the Institution of the Eucharist are inseparable from Jesus' Passion and death. It is all part of what we call his Paschal Mystery, the mystery that he is our Passover Lamb who is slain for the sake of our salvation. In the Eucharist, Jesus gives us the totality of himself: Body, Blood, Soul, and Divinity. He institutes this sacrament to be intimately and joyfully close to us. Similarly, in his Passion, he gives us the totality of himself by taking the suffering from our sin upon himself. He pours himself out entirely.

There is no love without suffering because love holds nothing back. If we shy away from suffering, it is because we are afraid to give ourselves fully and do not yet perfectly love. Jesus does not run from his suffering, even though he does not particularly want it. He prays fervently and with great anxiety for it to be taken away from him—but ultimately, in obedience to the Father, he embraces it because of the Father's will.

The mysterious thing is that we can meet God even in our sufferings. I tend to want to avoid even inconveniences and discomforts, let alone sufferings. I find myself internally or externally grumbling and complaining, blaming others and criticizing them because of some minor infraction of my preferences or will. When I do this, however, I miss the opportunity to meet God in the moment. I miss the chance to meet God in deep communion at the altar rail of the present, the altar rail of suffering. God is always present. He waits for us at each moment, as he does in the tabernacle, longing for us to come to him with faith.

Recently, I've been trying to make it my practice to embrace difficult things, especially inconvenient things, requests, jobs, and the like, because, in some mysterious way, God is present to me in those activities. Perhaps he meets me there because my intention is a bit purer. I'm definitely not doing these things because I want to do them or enjoy them—but I enjoy *him*.

In her diary, St. Gemma Galgani wrote that she had a vision of Christ crucified, and he said to her,

> Look, daughter, and learn to love. ... Do you see this Cross, these thorns, these nails, these bruises, these tears, these wounds,

this blood? They are all works of love and of infinite love. Do you see how much I have loved you? Do you really want to love me? Then first learn to suffer. It is by suffering that one learns to love.[17]

Jesus regularly gave St. Gemma a share in his agony, but after each time of suffering, she experienced so profound a sense of calm and consolation that she longed to suffer still further for Jesus.

It is in moments of suffering that we are able to be most closely united to Jesus and are best able to understand his infinite love for us. The Lord is always close to those who suffer. As we reflect on his suffering at the start of his Passion, let us unite our suffering to Jesus' and, through it, learn how to love yet more deeply.

## Respond

Instead of thinking of whether you could endure the maximum amount of suffering out of love, think of what your current limits are. What is a type of suffering that you struggle to endure but could push yourself to endure better, with God's help? What is something that currently seems difficult but eventually feasible? Next time that type of suffering comes around, do you think you could unite it with Christ's suffering on the Cross and endure it lovingly for him?

# Love

*Read Mark 15:1–41*

*"And when the centurion, who stood facing him, saw that he thus breathed his last, he said, 'Truly this man was the Son of God!'"*

## Reflect

I love the second chapter of St. Paul's letter to the Philippians, particularly where St. Paul talks about Christ's humility in becoming man and dying for us. I heard someone say that for one of us to choose to become a worm would be less of a descent, less of a humiliation, than for Jesus, the true God, to become incarnate as a man. For Jesus, the Lord of the living and the dead, the Word through whom and for whom everything exists, to be spat on the face while guilty are set free—for the eternal fire of consuming Love to be ridiculed by conceited hypocrites, only for him to respond with mercy and to pour his blood out for them as they rubbed it in his face—he could only have been lead to willingly undertake these things by the most quintessential form of love. How else can we respond to such love except with love and gratitude in return?

My friends once told me that, apparently, some women in labor get severe tunnel vision in the moment and have a sharpened, though limited, awareness of what's going on around them.

There are various theories for why this is. Some say it is so that when the baby is born, the mother can only focus on her infant. But my friends had a different thought; they believe (and have experienced personally) that their tunnel vision during labor is for the face of their spouse. While my friend was giving birth, her husband was right there, and all she could do was focus on his face, and he on hers. Yes, she is thinking of the coming baby—but she does this as an act of love for her husband, and he for her.

There is a connection here to Jesus' Passion: that his love for his Bride, the Church, got him through his suffering. In Hebrews 12:2, Paul says we run the race "while keeping our eyes fixed on Jesus, the leader and perfecter of faith. For the sake of the joy that lay before him he endured the cross, despising its shame, and has taken his seat at the right of the throne of God" (NAB). I like to think that the joy that was set before him was you and me, seated with him in heaven. The thought of you is what helped Jesus through his Passion. Perhaps the thought of him and the ultimate goal of heaven can help get you through your little sufferings today.

If you want an example of how to do this, look to Our Lady. I always find Good Friday difficult, but it helps for me to turn to Our Lady and walk through this day with her. Think of how she remained with Jesus right until the end, suffering so immensely along with him that her heart felt pierced with a sword—yet she never took her eyes off him. Her suffering was so inextricably united with his. She walks beside Jesus every step of the way, a sorrowful mother, praying and speaking encouragement. She is full of hope, full of confidence that, in him, God is reconciling us to himself and making all things new.

Let us go through this path of life and its sufferings with the same tunnel vision for Christ, with the same unshakeable confidence in him that leads us to profess with the faithful centurion: "Truly this man was the Son of God!" (Mark 15:39).

## Respond

Have a moment of quiet reflection today, meditating with sorrow on your sins. Thank Jesus not only for his sacrifice for you, but also for having saved you from the darkness of your sins that you committed despite that loving sacrifice. Reflect on the ways in which he has broken the shackles that bound you to particular sins, how he has freed you to live as a new creation in his love and mercy.

# Hope

*"He bought a linen shroud, and taking him down, wrapped him in the linen shroud, and laid him in a tomb which had been hewn out of the rock; and he rolled a stone against the door of the tomb."*

## Reflect

Holy Saturday is the most silent of days. It feels as if I can hear the realm of the dead trembling as it strives to contain the Uncontainable One. The first crack in hell's gates is sounded at Evening Prayer for Holy Saturday as we intone the First Antiphon: "Death, you shall die in me; Hell, you shall be destroyed in me."[18] What an epic line.

Holy Saturday is a day of silence, but it is also a day of hope. We're really good at hoping for Christmas during Advent. But our hope for Easter should be even sharper. Christian hope is not wishful thinking, such as, *Oh gosh, I hope Jesus makes it! I hope he wins!* We already know that he has triumphed over sin and death. Our hope, especially today, is a confident expectation in his total victory—that just as he indeed defeated death and shattered hell's gates, so too we confidently expect that he will work this total victory in us, that he will bring to completion in us all of the labors and prayers of Lent.

In the solemn silence of this Holy Saturday, we await the joy of celebrating Christ's Resurrection tomorrow. It's a small reflection of the entirety of our lives: We know Christ will come again, and we look forward in hope to the resurrection of the body when those who love him will be united with him fully, body and soul, in heaven. But until then, we wait with patient endurance.

Even when we know what the final chapter of the history of the world will look like, even when we know Jesus' triumph is certain, we sometimes don't understand the path he's leading us on to get to that point when that path is so strewn with suffering. It is in these moments of darkness that the virtue of hope comes to bear. As St. Paul tells us, "For in this hope we were saved. Now hope that is seen is not hope. For who hopes for what he sees? But if we hope for what we do not see, we wait for it with patience" (Romans 8:24–25). Hope keeps our end goal in sight so that, no matter what we are called to endure until then, we can trust that we will be united with God in the end.

Our Lady was suffused with hope as she waited for Jesus to rise. We wait with her and do as St. Paul tells us: "Rejoice in your hope, be patient in tribulation, be constant in prayer" (Romans 12:12). As we prepare to enter into this total victory liturgically in the Easter Vigil, let us stir up our hope into a fiery longing. I do this with the phrase, "Lord, I can't wait until …" So, we could pray, "Lord, I can't wait until I celebrate your Easter victory." In saying this, we're not just speaking of tonight and tomorrow or even for the whole Easter season. We're talking about spending all eternity with him in heaven.

## Respond

What things in your life are currently causing you confusion because you can't see God's hand at work behind them? As you think of those things, picture yourself standing before the stone rolled in front of Christ's tomb. Think of how, for all of Holy Saturday, the disciples couldn't see the joy of Easter because Christ lay hidden behind that stone. As you endure these moments in your own life, ask God to help you endure those times when you can't see him at work, when you feel like you're standing before the tomb. Ask him to increase the virtue of hope in you, to increase in you the confidence that he will bring about a resurrection in your heart.

*Easter*

SUNDAY

# Joy

*Read Mark 16:1–20*

"*Do not be amazed; you seek Jesus of Nazareth, who was crucified. He has risen, he is not here; see the place where they laid him.*"

## Reflect

The victory has been won. Jesus went to war on the Cross, but not in the conventional sense. He didn't come out guns a-blazing. Instead, he won by losing. He defeated Satan, death, sin, and hell by taking the beating of his life, to the point of losing his life—and then, as the Creed says, he descended into hell. But then Jesus stood up (in Greek, the word for resurrection, *anastasis*, literally means to stand up) and devastated his, and our, opponent.

The crazy thing about what we believe in Jesus' Resurrection is that Jesus did not just win this victory *for* us. Through our baptisms, we were with him; we were winning that battle in him, and he in us. We participate in this great victory of Christ's. We need to seize ownership of this birthright of ours because, although the war is won, the clean-up battles still rage until the end of time. Our time of fasting is over, but in the midst of our celebration, we make sure not to grow slack or give up all the practices we began this Lent. We know that these smaller battles rage on around us, so we don't throw out the spiritual armory we've been working so hard to build up.

It's equally important, though, to give joy its due season. In today's reading, Christ rebukes the eleven remaining apostles for their unbelief and hardness of heart. Their hearts were not receptive to the Easter tidings relayed to them by others. For us, then, let us affirm our belief in Christ's Resurrection and allow the joy of Easter to well up in our hearts and overflow into praise. St. Augustine writes,

> That [liturgical season] which is before Easter signifies tribulation, in which we now are; that which we are now keeping after Easter, signifies the bliss in which we shall hereafter be. The celebration then which we keep before Easter is what we do now: by that which we keep after Easter we signify what as yet we have not. Therefore we employ that time in fastings and prayer, this present time we spend in praises, and relax our fast. This is the Halleluia which we sing.[19]

Let us praise Jesus then for this victory over sin and death and celebrate what his Resurrection promises for us!

This Lent has been an epic journey, and I want to commend you for giving it your all. This is not an ending but rather a beginning. The day-to-day may look a little different, but I encourage you to shift gears as smoothly as possible, to keep the prayer schedule that you have discerned will work for you, along with whatever practices will help you fix your eyes on Jesus. You can't do it all, but whatever you do, do it for love of Christ and to get closer to him.

God bless you, and Happy Easter. Jesus is Risen! Alleluia!

## Respond

What are some of the fruits this Lent has borne for you? What practices do you want to maintain in order to see a continuation of that spiritual growth?

_____

_____

_____

_____

_____

_____

_____

_____

_____

_____

_____

_____

_____

_____

_____

_____

_____

_____

_____

_____

_____

_____

_____

_____

_____

_____

# DAILY CHALLENGE TRACKER

Lent is an opportunity to face physical and spiritual
challenges. Use this as a daily tracker to encourage
you to balance the needs of your body and soul
by participating in these Lenten challenges.

| DAY | DAILY WORKOUT | DIETARY FAST | SPIRITUAL READING | DAILY EXAMEN |
|-----|---------------|--------------|-------------------|--------------|
| 1   | ☐ | ☐ | ☐ | ☐ |
| 2   | ☐ | ☐ | ☐ | ☐ |
| 3   | ☐ | ☐ | ☐ | ☐ |
| 4   | ☐ | ☐ | ☐ | ☐ |
| 5   | ☐ | ☐ | ☐ | ☐ |
| 6   | ☐ | ☐ | ☐ | ☐ |
| 7   | ☐ | ☐ | ☐ | ☐ |
| 8   | ☐ | ☐ | ☐ | ☐ |
| 9   | ☐ | ☐ | ☐ | ☐ |
| 10  | ☐ | ☐ | ☐ | ☐ |
| 11  | ☐ | ☐ | ☐ | ☐ |
| 12  | ☐ | ☐ | ☐ | ☐ |
| 13  | ☐ | ☐ | ☐ | ☐ |
| 14  | ☐ | ☐ | ☐ | ☐ |
| 15  | ☐ | ☐ | ☐ | ☐ |
| 16  | ☐ | ☐ | ☐ | ☐ |

| | | | | |
|---|---|---|---|---|
| 17 | ☐ | ☐ | ☐ | ☐ |
| 18 | ☐ | ☐ | ☐ | ☐ |
| 19 | ☐ | ☐ | ☐ | ☐ |
| 20 | ☐ | ☐ | ☐ | ☐ |
| 21 | ☐ | ☐ | ☐ | ☐ |
| 22 | ☐ | ☐ | ☐ | ☐ |
| 23 | ☐ | ☐ | ☐ | ☐ |
| 24 | ☐ | ☐ | ☐ | ☐ |
| 25 | ☐ | ☐ | ☐ | ☐ |
| 26 | ☐ | ☐ | ☐ | ☐ |
| 27 | ☐ | ☐ | ☐ | ☐ |
| 28 | ☐ | ☐ | ☐ | ☐ |
| 29 | ☐ | ☐ | ☐ | ☐ |
| 30 | ☐ | ☐ | ☐ | ☐ |
| 31 | ☐ | ☐ | ☐ | ☐ |
| 32 | ☐ | ☐ | ☐ | ☐ |
| 33 | ☐ | ☐ | ☐ | ☐ |
| 34 | ☐ | ☐ | ☐ | ☐ |
| 35 | ☐ | ☐ | ☐ | ☐ |
| 36 | ☐ | ☐ | ☐ | ☐ |
| 37 | ☐ | ☐ | ☐ | ☐ |
| 38 | ☐ | ☐ | ☐ | ☐ |
| 39 | ☐ | ☐ | ☐ | ☐ |
| 40 | ☐ | ☐ | ☐ | ☐ |

| | | | | |
|---|---|---|---|---|
| 41 | ☐ | ☐ | ☐ | ☐ |
| 42 | ☐ | ☐ | ☐ | ☐ |
| 43 | ☐ | ☐ | ☐ | ☐ |
| 44 | ☐ | ☐ | ☐ | ☐ |
| 45 | ☐ | ☐ | ☐ | ☐ |
| 46 | ☐ | ☐ | ☐ | ☐ |
| 47 | ☐ | ☐ | ☐ | ☐ |

# NOTES

1. Thérèse of Lisieux, "Letters Of Saint Thérèse To Her Sister Celine" (October 20, 1888), *Paths of Love*, pathsoflove.com.

2. C. S. Lewis, *Mere Christianity* (Samizdat, 2014), 32.

3. Thérèse of Lisieux, *Story of a Soul* (ICS Publications, 1996), 195.

4. Jim Graves, "'He Leadeth Me': 9 Things to Know About Father Walter Ciszek, a 20th-Century Catholic Hero," *National Catholic Register*, ncregister.com.

5. Teresa of Calcutta, "Nobel Peace Prize 1979: Acceptance Speech," *The Nobel Prize*, nobelprize.org.

6. Thomas à Kempis, *The Imitation of Christ*, trans. Fr. Dylan Schrader (Ascension, 2025), 158.

7. John Paul II, "Letter to Families - *Gratissimam Sane*" (1994), vatican.va.

8. Bonaventure, "The Life of St. Francis" (1260), quoted in *Bonaventure: The Soul's Journey into God; The Tree of Life; The Life of St. Francis*, trans. Ewert H. Cousins, *The Classics of Western Spirituality* (Paulist Press, 1978), 263, archive.org.

9. George Pollard, "The Revelation of the Sacred Heart of Jesus Paralle-Monial, France," *EWTN*, ewtn.com.

10. John Chrysostom, "Homily 8 on Philippians," *New Advent*, newadvent.org.

11. Chrysostom, "Homily 8 on Philippians."

12. C. S. Lewis, *The Four Loves* (Geoffrey Bles, 1960), 73.

13. "Prayer of Saint Teresa of Ávila," *EWTN*, ewtn.com.

14. Teresa of Ávila, *The Life of St. Teresa of Jesus, of the Order of Our Lady of Carmel*, trans. David Lewis (1888), XI.6, ccel.org.

15. Faustina Kowalska, *Diary: Divine Mercy in My Soul* (Krakow: Misericordia Publications, 2019), 439 (para. 866), saint-faustina.org.

16. "Minute Meditations - The Pardon Prayer," *Franciscan Media*, franciscanmedia.org.

17. Gemma Galgani, *The Diary of St. Gemma* (Sophia Institute Press, 2022), 77.

18. "Holy Saturday - Evening Prayer," *The Liturgy Archive*, liturgies.net.

19. Augustine, "Exposition on Psalm 148," *New Advent*, newadvent.org.

# ABOUT THE AUTHOR

A native of County Kildare, Ireland, **Fr. Columba Jordan** is a Franciscan Friar of the Renewal (CFR) currently serving in St. Patrick's Friary, Limerick. His main ministry is youth work in addition to his work as a popular speaker and presenter. He hosts the weekly video podcast, *Little By Little*, offering short-form faith formation.

# PROGRAM CREDITS

**Executive Producer**
Jonathan Strate

**General Managers**
Jeffrey Cole, Lauren McCann

**Product Manager**
Madelynn Felix

**Project Manager**
Rebecca Cabell

**Editorial**
Christina Eberle, Melayna Alicea

**Graphics**
Stella Ziegler

**Marketing**
Annie Elfelt

The Ascension App is the
# #1 Catholic Bible App

Thank you for choosing *Crux: Daily Lenten Meditations* to accompany you this Lent. We pray it has been a spiritually fruitful season.

If you wish to continue on your *Crux* journey, the Ascension App has many great features that can assist you, such as the Daily Examen, reflection prompts and questions, and optional reminders to help you build a daily habit of prayer.

Scan the QR code
to download and
begin exploring the
Ascension App.

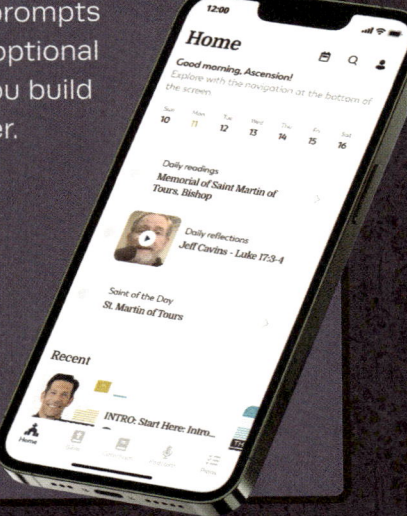